Lady Suzanne Miller

OMENS, CURSES
and
SUPERSTITIONS
How to REMOVE and
REVERSE them. . .

INNER LIGHT PUBLICATIONS
New Brunswick, NJ

OMENS, CURSES AND
SUPERSTITIONS: HOW TO REMOVE
AND REVERSE THEM
by Lady Suzanne Miller

ISBN: 1-892062-02-X

Editorial Direction: Timothy Green Beckley

Special thanks to Tim Swartz, Carol Ann Rodriguez
and Clementine B. Graham

For permission to reprint specific portions or to inquire
about foreign rights, address request to Inner Light,
Box 753, New Brunswick, NJ 08903

FREE CATALOG UPON REQUEST

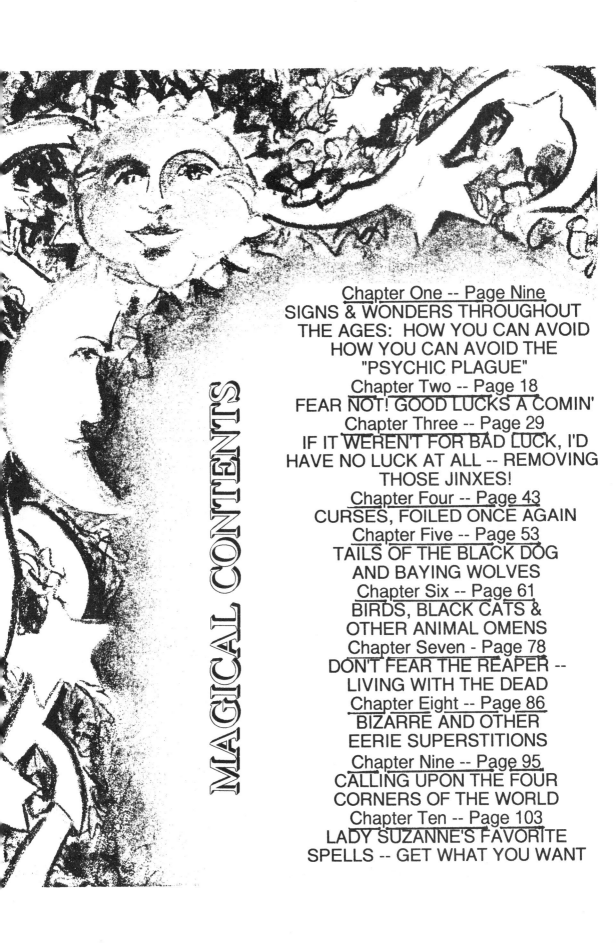

MAGICAL CONTENTS

Psychic, Lady Suzanne Miller

OMENS, CURSES & SUPERSTITIONS

INTRODUCTION

IS IT ANY WONDER THERE ARE SIGNS AND WONDERS?

By Timothy Green Beckley

What gives you the right to think you are so unlucky? Does it have anything at all to do with the fact that the cards never come up the right suit; that the dice always fall where they may (which is not how you placed your bet); or that the beer guzzling, chain smoker down the hall has won the Pick Six three weeks in a row?

Well lady Suzanne Miller is here to tell you not to fret child . . . that luck will surely cometh your way soon and that every cloud almost assuredly does have a silver lining, though we may at times have to poke and prod it a bit in order for the sun to shine just a wee bit.

One thing Suzanne has learned as a long time practicing psychic and magician, is that sometimes matters must be helped along. Even in nature you can't expect something for nothing my good friend. For every positive there is usually a negative; for every yin, a yang; and its often a matter of simply drawing upon that "positive flow" and not having it bounce off the walls around you.

Once you've learned the occult "facts of life," YOUR life will turn about. Things will begin to change before your eyes and will get much rosier - - get the picture?

Now, I've known Suzanne since the early 1970's when she wandered into my School of Occult Arts and Sciences on 14th Street in Manhattan, where some of today's "big wigs" in the metaphysical world got their start. Even in her early twenties, she was a whiz at anything to do with the supernatural, and I know that since those days she's made an even deeper study of omens, curses, and superstitions - - or you wouldn't be able to buy this book today.

As far as I can tell, every nationality - - every culture - - every society - - has its own omens and curses; some of them are well known, others have to be hunted down and discovered despite the mixing and mingling of years of telling and retelling.

You can be certain that Suzanne has done her homework and with a few of the spells she's added as a bonus at the back of this book, you should be sailing along toward that cloud with a silver lining with the very next breeze.

If you ask my opinion (as a practicing parapsychologist and a historian of the occult), when it comes to the subject of the material in this book, it's rather difficult - - and not even necessary - - to be overly concerned about the source of its origin. After all, normally we take the word of people we meet all the time and we hardly even know enough about them to know how reliable they might be in any circumstance. Who is to know how reliable they might be in any circumstance. Who takes the time to dare question a person's faith in God or a superior being, or what happened to them an hour ago? So why dampen their spirits when it comes to their superstitious beliefs?

Some of what Suzanne has related might be classified as "whoppers," but who's to make a final decision on the accuracy of others? If you want, you can take what you read here with a pinch of salt (something she recommends in these pages anyway); or you can take what you are told at face value.

Many of the stories are meant to be taken literally . . . others, perhaps not so much so . . .

OMENS, CURSES & SUPERSTITIONS

The following is a prime example of what I am referring to. It was related by a women of Greek extraction concerning her great-grandmother whom she always loved dearly (after all, would granny have it in her soul to be a liar?). We can only report what we're told in the lady's own words - - for after all, what gives society the right to be judgmental over what others confess to?

Her story:

"My great-grandmother was known as a 'grannie woman.' In the days before cars and other forms of transportation, folks often didn't have easy access to a doctor or hospital. That's where my great-grandmother came in handy. She had the ability to stop bleeding, often at a distance. Now I know that doesn't sound like much. However, in those days, working on the farm offered numerous dangers for human and farm animal alike. Injuries could lead to massive bleeding and probable death.

" Great granny had several ways to stop bleeding. One way was to drape a spider's web over the wound. Another way involved cases where she couldn't attend to the patient personally. She would lock herself away in her room with a Bible, after about an hour she would come out and announce that the patient's bleeding had stopped. Generally word would soon arrive that indeed, the victim's bleeding had stopped at the time granny said.

"For some reason granny had trouble doing her long-distance cures if there was water, especially a creek or river, between her and her patient. She had no explanation, maybe the water would 'carry' her spell down stream and away from her charge. She just knew that water interfered with her cures."

Regardless of whether or not you're superstitious - - or believe in signs and omens. I can guarantee you'll learn a lot from the material Suzanne has collected; and no doubt will obtain knowledge of some of the things you should avoid on the path to a more prosperous, richer, more fulfilling life. I am happy to be able to present this work on her behalf.

Timothy Green Beckley
INNER LIGHT PUBLICATIONS

P.S. We welcome your own contributions for a future edition and ask that you send them to us at: **Superstitions** c/o Inner Light Publications Box, 753 New Brunswick, NJ   08903

Chapter One:
SIGNS & WONDERS
THROUGHOUT THE AGES:
HOW YOU CAN AVOID
THE "PSYCHIC PLAGUE"

OMENS, CURSES & SUPERSTITIONS

In days gone by, people were more aware of the world around them. They were keen observers of the changes of weather, of unusual behavior in animals, and of the spiritual world that surrounded them. Over the centuries people passed down these observations in the form of omens, portents, superstitions, and other forms of natural magic.

Some people became experts at reading and interpreting these signs. They became the shamans and holy ones, the healers and curse makers. They evoked both fear and respect from their peers. These secrets were passed down from generation to generation, each holder would add to the store of knowledge so that the next in line would know just a little bit more about the truths of the world.

Nowadays we have the privilege to have access to much of what was considered secret in the past. These secrets have been given to us in the form of folk tales, sayings, and old-time spells. Stuff that any old granny woman worth her salt would have known and jealously guarded from the common folk. After all, what good is a secret if everybody knows it.

Many modern cultures disregard signs and miracles. Within some religious circles there is a common notion that miracles stopped at the time of the New Testament. Thus, omens, which are like miracles at times, are relegated to old wive's tales and superstitions.

You hear about some of these old wive's tales such as: Never walk under a ladder, or beware of a black cat that is crossing your path, or break a mirror and you have seven years bad luck. How about fold money towards yourself and more will come soon. (I hear someone making note of that one!)

The original meanings have been forgotten. I would speculate that, centuries ago, a black cat crossed someone's path, and a tragedy occurred in that person's life. An observant reader of signs took note of it and then watched for that sign again. It happened that a similar situation again occurred and with similar results. A rule was born. Be careful of rules, but be open to interpretations and possibilities.

Remember to keep the options, the interpretations, open and fluid. Look for an individual interpretation, not an all-encompassing meaning. Watch out, too, for wishful thinking. There is the story of the ancient Greek King that was going to do battle with the Persians. He went to a famous temple and asked the oracle to prophesy for him. The oracle told him that if he went to battle the Persian King, a great empire would fall. This was the news he was waiting for. He gathered his army together and attacked the Persians. He lost. The oracle was right. A great empire did fall, his. It was a matter of interpretation.

Some bad omens can even be removed or reversed quite easily as far as I'm concerned. The following are two good examples of what I've personally found to be the case.

- When a black cat crosse my path, I literally back up and take another path. Of course these days some black cats just run when they see me coming, as my friends can testify. Saves on gas too! I've also owned many black cats and I think it only counts if it's a strange black cat.

- When you break a mirror as long as you don't see yourself in it, bad luck is averted. Also if you drop one just turn your glance away and you'll be fine.

Since the beginning, man has always looked for signs that would predict future events. From these signs came the belief in superstitions and omens. The actual meaning of superstition is "the blind use of a form whose significance has been forgotten." The definition of an omen is "a rare or extraordinary event or physical activity using a non-human agency to prognosticate an emotional event." Simply put, an omen is something out of the ordinary that lets you know something important is going to happen.

ORACLES AND AUGERS

Today we have psychics to help us interpret our lives. These modern psychics have roots that can be traced all the way back to the oracles and augers from ancient times. For those of you who have never heard of an auger - well, an auger was part of a group of ancient Roman officials charged with observing and interpreting omens for guidance in public affairs.

The observation, collection, and study of divine omens was an important function of the Roman state. The state religion dictated that gods intervened in human affairs, and the very proof of this was the "elaborate procedures for interpreting events which might indicate divine will." This point was made by Cicero in his treatise on omens, *De Divinatione*. While Cicero challenges divination in his study of Roman philosophy, he acknowledges that omens tended to be classified according to which priests interpreted them. This suggests that these "elaborate procedures" were indeed a vital form of devotion to the gods, a form which assumed that omens were, in fact, divinely sanctioned.

For instance, the night before Caesar was assassinated, there were a lot of unusual sightings interpreted as omens. There were things like meteors, bad storms, and vultures where there shouldn't have been vultures. All signifying to those in the know that something big was going to happen. Beware the Ides of March.

The different types of messages from the gods consisted of Auspices, which were

OMENS, CURSES & SUPERSTITIONS

a form of divination used to consult the gods' opinion prior to a new undertaking. These were: Roman augury, the study of birds' activities, and extipicy, the study of animal entrails. Usually the liver and gall-bladders of sheep. A form of divination that I am happy to say has fallen out of favor in modern times.

Prodigies were signs, supernatural events, and manifestations of the paranormal which were reported to the senate and carefully collected in lists each year, according to a specific set of procedures. They were unasked-for messages from the gods and therefore a very grave matter, more often than not a warning or expression of divine displeasure.

Omens were spontaneous dreams and prophesies, often referring to a specific undertaking or person. Omens, unlike auspicium, were not merely messages stating the gods' will on a particular matter, but were spontaneous glimpses into the future. They often provided details on fate, often in the very Roman sense of "to meet one's fate," that is, one's doom.

IT'S ALL GREEK TO ME

In ancient Greece, we learned from Socrates lessons to Plato: "You have heard me speak at sundry times and in diverse places of an oracle or sign which comes to me. This sign, which is a kind of voice, first began to come to me when I was a child. It always warns but never commands me to do anything which I am going to do."

The Greeks took the will of the gods into serious consideration. They consciously used their understanding of a greater power, sometimes called Fate, even in their voting. The ancient Greeks loved contests of all sorts. In their theatrical contests, which went on for days, they included a unique way for the gods to vote. They took out half of the ballots and tossed them into the air. Fate, chance, or the will of the gods, had their say. (Could you imagine our modern elections doing that?)

A CHINESE THEORY OF PORTENTS

It is believed that Tung Chung-shu lived in ancient China around 179?-104? B.C. He spent a large portion of his life writing down his observations dealing with signs and portents. The title of his finished work from which the following selection is taken translates as: ***Deep Significance of the Spring and Autumn Annals.***

"The creatures of Heaven and earth at times display unusual changes and these are called wonders. Lesser ones are called ominous portents. The portents always come first and are followed by wonders. Portents are Heaven's warnings, wonders are Heaven's threats. Heaven first sends warnings, and if men do not understand, then it sends wonders to awe them. This is what the Book of Odes means when it says: 'We tremble at the awe and the fearfulness of Heaven!'

"The genesis of all such portents and wonders is a direct result of errors in the state. When the first indications of error begin to appear in the state, Heaven sends forth ominous portents and calamities to warn men and announce the fact. If, in spite of these warnings and announcements, men still do not realize how they have gone wrong, then Heaven sends prodigies and wonders to terrify them. If, after these terrors, men still know no awe or fear, then calamity and misfortune will visit them. From this we may see that the will of Heaven is benevolent, for it has no desire to trap or betray mankind.

"If we examine these wonders and portents carefully, we may discern the will of Heaven. The will of Heaven desires us to do certain things and not to do others. As to those things which Heaven wishes and does not wish, if a man searches within himself, he will surely find warnings of them in his own heart, and if he looks about him

14

at daily affairs, he will find verification of these warnings in the state.

"Thus we can discern the will of Heaven in these portents and wonders. We should not hate such signs, but stand in awe of them, considering that Heaven wishes to repair our faults and save us from our errors. Therefore it takes this way to warn us.

THE APPEARANCE OF A WHITE PHEASANT

A Favorable omen in ancient Japan

The Emperor said: "When a sage ruler appears in the world and rules the Empire, Heaven is responsive to him, and manifests favorable omens. In ancient times, during the reign of Ch'eng-wang of the Chou Dynasty, a ruler of the Western land (China), and again in the time of Ming Ti of the Han Dynasty, white pheasants were seen.

"In this Our Land of Japan, during the reign of the Emperor Homuda, a white crow made its nest in the Palace. In the time of the Emperor 0-sazaki, a Dragon-horse appeared in the West. This shows that from ancient times until now, there have been many cases of auspicious omens appearing in response to virtuous rulers. What we call phoenixes, unicorns, white pheasants, white crows, and such like birds and beasts, even including herbs and trees, in short all things having the property of significant response, are favorable omens and auspicious signs produced by Heaven and Earth.

"Now that wise and enlightened sovereigns should obtain such auspicious omens is neat and proper. But why should We, who are so empty and shallow, have this good fortune? It is no doubt wholly due to Our Assistants, the Ministers, imperial Chieftains, Deity Chieftains, Court Chieftains and Local Chieftains, each of whom, with the utmost loyalty, conforms to the regulations that are made. For this reason, let us, from the Ministers down to the functionaries, with pure hearts reverence the Gods of Heaven

OMENS, CURSES & SUPERSTITIONS

and Earth, and one and all accepting the glad omen, make the Empire to flourish."

Again he commanded, saying: "The provinces and districts in the four quarters having been placed in Our charge by Heaven, We exercise supreme rule over the Empire. Now in the province of Anato, ruled over by Our divine ancestors, this auspicious omen has appeared. For this reason We proclaim a general amnesty throughout the Empire, and begin a new year-period, to be called White Pheasant. Moreover We prohibit the flying of falcons within the limits of the province of Anato."

OMENS FORETELL AZTEC DOOM

In the spring of 1519 a Spanish expedition of eleven ships set sail from Cuba. On board were 508 soldiers, 16 horses, and several pieces of artillery. The first land they sighted was the coast of Yucatán, once the heart of the Mayan empire. The leader of this small Spanish band was a young adventurer named Hernán Cortés. Little did he realize that his arrival coincided precisely with the foreseen return of the Plumed Serpent. On Holy Thursday, Cortés moored his ships off the Mexican coast and founded the city of Veracruz in the name of the Emperor Charles.

Another emperor, named Montezuma, received the news. "The gods have come back. Their lances spit fire. Their warriors have two heads and six legs, and they live in houses that float." The whole Aztec empire was filled with foreboding, as comets raced across the sky in broad daylight.

The fall of the Aztecs came to no surprise to the ancient prophets who had forecast in the ancient books of memory. "Prepare yourselves, oh my little brothers, for the white twin of heaven has come and he will castrate the sun, bringing the night and sadness and the weight of pain."

OMENS, CURSES & SUPERSTITIONS

Ten years before the arrival of the Spaniards, omens were seen which seemed to foretell calamities in the future:

- Every night for a year a flame appeared in the eastern sky which continued till dawn.

- For no explainable reason, the temple of Huitzilopochtli at Tlacateccan burned down. The temple of Xiuhtecuhtli at Tzonmolco was struck by lightning.

- A comet which broke into three parts appeared during the day.

- The waters of Lake Tezcoco boiled up and destroyed the surrounding houses.

- The voice of a woman was heard at night crying, "My dear children, we have to go! Where can I take you?"

- A brown crane was captured by some fishermen and brought to Motecuhzoma. The crest of the bird was shaped like a mirror in which Motecuhzoma saw the heavens and what appeared to be an army riding on deer-like animals.

Cortés finally vanquished the Aztec capital after a bloody siege in 1521. The last Aztec poet cried out in his despair: "Where shall we go now, oh my friends? The smoke is rising, the fog is spreading, the waters on the lake are red. Cry, for we have lost the Aztec nation." As foretold by the omens, the time of the fifth sun was at an end.

Chapter Two:
FEAR NOT!
GOOD LUCKS
A COMIN'

OMENS, CURSES & SUPERSTITIONS

"Good and ill luck," says the French philosopher, Montaigne, "are in my opinion sovereign powers. It is absurd to think that human prudence is able to act the same part as fortune will do." Shakespeare says: "There's a divinity that shapes our ends, rough-hew them how we will."

The belief in the power of some object or some act to produce a change in one's fortunes for better or for worse, is inherent in the human race. There are few words in our language that have such a universal appeal as LUCK. Luck may be defined as chance, or if a person is religious, as Providence. Either way, we all go through some pretty elaborate means to insure our good luck. From crossing our fingers to spitting three times, the methods of finding and holding good luck are as numerous and varied as the stars in the sky. And sometimes just as elusive.

Knock On Wood

One of the most prevalent customs is the touching or knocking on wood for good luck or to ward off evil. Its origin has been lost to the ages, though some think that it can be traced back to the ancient religious rite of touching a crucifix when taking an oath.

In Europe, it was widely believed that trees housed all sorts of sprites and fairies. To knock on wood was suppose to acknowledge their existance and ask their assistance to grant wishes and keep away evil. Nowadays, wood has often been replaced with plastic and other man-made materials. Saying "knock on Formica" just doesn't have the same appeal.

To brag about good health or success, according to the general belief, invites the envy of the powers of evil, and to counteract this you must, according to some authorities, touch wood. In fact, just to be safe, you should knock on wood three times.

OMENS, CURSES & SUPERSTITIONS

I guess to get the attention of the wood spirits in case they weren't paying attention.

Charms made of wood are often worn on watch chains so that the wearer may have and article handy for the purpose of knocking. This practice has led to other superstitions, such as fondling a gold watch chain in the belief that the touch of gold will insure success. I wonder if gold plate would work as well?

Sir Walter Scott, while a student at college, always fumbled with a wooden button which was attached to his coat. This brought him success in his tests. It is told that when his fellow students secretly cut off the button, Scott was so flustered on discovering its absence, that he failed hopelessly and was sent to the end of his class. With friends like that, who needs enemies?

Other signs of Luck

■ Seeing the new moon first over the left shoulder.

■ Picking up a horseshoe on the road.

■ Picking up a four leaf clover.

■ Seeing two black crows flying overhead.

OMENS, CURSES & SUPERSTITIONS

- A spider found crawling on a person is good luck.

- Putting on a garment inside out by mistake.

- Picking up a coin.

- Picking up a pin or a white button.

- A rooster crowing on the doorstep.

- To see a baby smiling in its sleep.

- To dream of one's father.

- A bee coming into the room.

Bees are symbols of the Goddess. However, where I come from, a bee flying into the room is a sure sign that everybody's going to be getting the hell out as soon as possible. Maybe the good luck is for the bee who now has the room all to its self.

Another good luck charm is the rabbit's foot. Like the old joke, if it was so lucky what happened to the original owner? Thats not my idea of good luck. A horseshoe hung above the front door is considered lucky for all who enter. Just make sure you hang the shoe with the open ends facing up, lest the luck runs out and makes a mess.

OMENS, CURSES & SUPERSTITIONS

Lucky Money

Many people would say that having lots of money is lucky. While others say just the opposite - Money is the root of all evil. However, money, especially coins, have been used as good luck charms for centuries. Lucky pennies or other coins are carried around by many individuals. It is believed that they drive away evil influences in business and bring luck in money matters.

Often silver coins are stamped with the cross or other religious symbols to insure good luck. If you find a penny face up, put it in your pocket to insure success for the rest of the day. However, if you find a penny face down, leave it be to keep evil away. Put a peso or other coins in various corners of your new home for good luck. Throw coins around your house on New Years for good luck. If someone hands you some pennies, throw them back over your head, and you won't lose your luck.

Put a coin in a purse or wallet, when giving either as a gift. Supposedly, this breaks any bad luck concerning finances for the receiver. As for myself, I consider it good luck if someone puts tens and twenties in my purse. This definitely insures that bad luck in finances will be kept away, at least for a little while.

I personally subscribe to at least two money drawing beliefs:

- Bill wrappers' should be saved and not thrown away because they will attract more money.

- Put a buckeye wrapped with a dollar bill in a green bag in your pocket or purse and you'll never be broke.

OMENS, CURSES & SUPERSTITIONS

If your left palm itches, this is a sign of money coming your way. Recently, I returned from a trip and while I was away, my left palm itched continually. On arriving home, I won $580.00 on the daily lottery and two days later, $80.00 more. This has happened to me on several occasions.

A feather flying by you means someone will steal your money. Always burn your onion peelings and you will never be empty-handed. Always pick up the burnt matches that you see and you will find money, as well as making the world a little cleaner.

As soon as you see a shooting star, say, "Money, money, money" and you will get money. Bubbles in falling rain mean you will get a lot of money, and wet. By wearing a dime in each shoe on New Year's Day you will have money all year. Carry a gold coin for luck, the trick is being able to afford one in the first place.

Carrying pennies in your pocket will make you unlucky. Do not spend a coin that someone gives you on New Year's day and you will have money all year. Drive a nail into a post to secure money. Finding an empty purse will bring success, except for the person who lost it.

Hang a man's socks up by the tops and you will be able to keep your money. This doesn't say if the man must remain in the socks for this to work. Hold up a piece of money to the new moon and you will receive money, and here I've been wasting my time going to the ATM.

If you wear a dime in your shoe you will never be unlucky, just uncomfortable. It causes bad luck to carry three dollars. It is lucky to put money in the foundation of a building. Just before midnight on New Year's Eve set a tub of water out in the yard and into it drop a penny and you will be lucky in money matters for the next year.

OMENS, CURSES & SUPERSTITIONS

On first seeing the new moon, look at it over your right shoulder if there is money in your pocket, and you will always have money; or have money until the next new moon. The one finding a dime in a birthday cake will be rich, especially after the lawsuit. To secure good luck, carry a penny or coin that was minted in the year of your birth.

You will never be without money, if you wear a little bag containing red pepper. You will never lose money, if you carry a coin, especially an old coin. You will have bad luck if you accept a two dollar bill.

Luck at Gambling

The late movie star Betty Grable was an avid gambler and also was very superstitious. While gambling, she thought her luck would change if she rubbed the dice or blew on them or if she changed her seat, used good luck charms or changed the deck of cards.

She did not like a hat put on a bed. She had a real fear of hats, shoes and umbrellas. She did like hats in a closet shelf with shoes. She would always put her left shoe on before the right. If a pair of shoes ended upon a table, she threw them out.

She never wanted her friends to wish her good luck and whistling in her dressing room was not allowed. Also, she did not like anyone to take anything from her hand. As she never received spiritual guidance form her mother, superstitions allayed her fears of which she had many.

Her sister said that Grable believed in ghosts and actually believed she shared a mysterious bond with them. She believed that her house in Los Angeles had "ghosts" in it. The bricks were from a castle in England. Grable believed that ghosts had come with the bricks to haunt her house. She later sold the house to Carol Burnett.

Grable was also a believer in the occult and numerology. There's an old superstition that death comes in threes. The movie industry thought of this when Grable passed away, then Veronica Lake shortly afterwards and a week later, Susan Hayward.

Bingo players also have a wide range of beliefs in lucky charms. I have seen players bring all sorts of small trinkets to bingo games. Some have small Buddhas, ceramic elephants, etc., even small photos of grandchildren set in front of them while playing insures good fortune. Lets not forget about the troll dolls, or wishniks as they were called in my days. Many bingo players have a number of large and small troll dolls to guarantee a winning night.

Here are some other interesting superstitions about gambling. Try some of them out, that is if you're feeling lucky.

- A gambler will never take a two-dollar bill unless you tear off the corner.

- A good gambler never uses the same deck of cards twice.

- A man standing by you in a dice game is always bad luck, unless he is in the game.

- Good poker players always sit with one foot over the other.

OMENS, CURSES & SUPERSTITIONS

■ You will be lucky at poker, if you borrow the money you play with.

■ If before eleven o'clock in the morning you boast about winning a game that afternoon, your side will be defeated.

■ If you are going to gamble, strike a match and if it burns to the end, you will be lucky; if it breaks off, don't gamble that day.

■ Remember that luck only lasts a few minutes and then is gone for a long time.

Amulets and Precious Stones

An amulet is also known as a fetish, talisman or charm. It may be an artifact such as a wood carving or a natural object such as a precious stone or shell. Some amulets bear religious images or texts whereas others have astrological significance.

In the 15th century, amulets were discovered being worn by west-coast Africans, however, the belief in amulets is thought to originate in man's prehistoric past. They are believed to hold the power of the sacred. Amulets are portable so that they are always accessible to the bearer. Individuals wear amulets to ward off ill effects or they may even be given to loved ones as get well charms and are to be kept on the body at all times.

OMENS, CURSES & SUPERSTITIONS

Power of Precious Stones

Agate: An agate is a precious translucent stone. According to ancient superstitions, wearing agate made one persuasive, agreeable, prudent and bold. It brought God's favor and bestowed the power to vanquish enemies and acquire riches.

Amber: A fossilized resin that is a favorite of witches. It is used for healing and protection and is also very lucky. When rubbed it produces an electrical charge.

Beads: Certain cultures and religions believe that beads serve as an additional function involving superstition or magic. They are thought to bring good luck, to ward off evil, or attract the attention of a deity so that he might watch over a person but only when taken in possession. Strung beads are used for counting prayers in some religions such as Buddhism.

Diamond: Diamond engagement rings were given by medieval Italians, because of their belief that the diamond was created from the flames of love. In France, it was thought that a diamond held against the forehead of an insane person would cure the ailment.

Emerald: The emerald supposedly soothes the eyes, preserves chastity, cures dysentery, prevents epilepsy, drives away evil spirits and helps childbirth. The horseshoe and other iron objects are also used as amulets. Others include good luck charms such as rabbit's foot, blue beads used in Islamic countries, stones, horns, bones, figurines, coins and medallions.

Jet: A cousin of coal, very light in weight but very black in color. Another favorite of witches. Very protective substance alternated with amber to form very powerful protective necklaces worn by many powerful Wise Women. Also jet can be used for scrying very effectively as it presents a smooth black surface.

Opal: The opal is said to threaten stability and bring misfortune, unless you were born under the sign of Libra, then it is lucky. Queen Maria Cristina of Spain refused to wear a particular opal because it had been owned by a Bourbon family in which no less than five unexplained deaths had occurred. Opals are reputed to strengthen sight, cure eye diseases, and to make the wearer invisible.

Pearl: Pearls are associated with tears and sorrow. Pearls are thought to indicate by changing colors, the condition of the wearer. It was believed that sickness would produce one color and imminent death another. Giving a pearl to a newborn child ensures them a long life.

Ruby: The wearers of rubies are likely to be passionate and deep lovers. The jewel imparts a high voltage charge to any affair. The red ruby was believed to insure good luck because the color would frighten away the devil and evil in general.

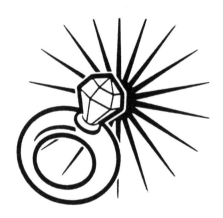

Chapter Three:
IF IT WEREN'T FOR BAD LUCK, I'D HAVE NO LUCK AT ALL -- REMOVING THOSE JINXES!

OMENS, CURSES & SUPERSTITIONS

The fear of bad luck has never troubled me very much. I have known a lot of sorrow in my life, but then again who hasn't? However, I seem to be incapable of reading random bad chance as the work of enemies or evil spirits. I search for good luck, and yet, to tell the truth, many people do feel the jinx, the curse, the bad luck spell on their trail.

Worse still, some people seek to place the jinx on others; luck is not enough for them; they want to force others to do their will (like most politicians). To this end they may use amulets, charms, and talismans, augmented by oils, incense, and candles. Because of this belief, a vast number of bad luck "remedies" has been prescribed over the years.

Apotropaic charms, those which repel accidental or intentional evil, are by definition never "lucky." Instead, their purpose is to keep bad luck at bay. That would then leave room for the "good luck" to fill the niche vacated by the bad luck. The evil eye belief, especially, has spawned a host of protective amulets. Disease has also built a ready market in apotropaic charms. The vagaries of travel, war, and other unsettling conditions leads to the use of lucky charms.

Certain actions are also believed to foster bad luck. Breaking a mirror, walking under a ladder, stepping on a crack. These all indicate that bad luck is thought of as almost some kind of malevolent entity, ready to pounce on those who would unknowingly break the "laws of the universe."

Attracting Bad Luck

Many people will not open an umbrella inside a house or building, this is considered to bring bad luck. Especially if the umbrella is held over the head. You are not suppose to sew on a Sunday. People believed it to be the beginning of a week, that included disappointments and setbacks.

Never move back into an apartment you previously lived in. When placing clothing on a bed, do not place the clothes lengthwise or overhanging. This indicates a person may become ill or be in failing health. To drop a glove means disappointment.

Pisbog

Years ago, an elderly Irish woman was heard to remark that a whistling girl comes to no good. I used to worry about that often as I was always a whistler as a young girl. I seem to have come out alright though.

Pisbog is Irish for superstitions and should be avoided for reasons of attracting negativity. Take these examples I have learned:

- Never under any circumstance should you take a picture of a pregnant woman or take her to a cemetery, or you might expose her to spirit possession of the unborn baby.

- Black cat unharmed crossing your path is good luck.

- If it just looks at you it's bad luck. If you run over it, it's very bad luck.

OMENS, CURSES & SUPERSTITIONS

Other signs of bad luck:

- Having thirteen people at a table

- Coiling a rope against the sun

- Purchasing a broom in May

- If you step on a grave, if you carry anything (flowers, etc.) out of a graveyard, if the item does not belong to you .

- Hold your breath when going by a cemetery to keep from breathing in disembodied spirits.

- If you desecrate or damage a cemetery in any way.

- If a gravedigger does not stay to see the grave filled and covered.

- If you collide with a hearse or stop a funeral procession.

- If you see a funeral procession. If you count the cars, worse still.

- Meeting a red haired women. (Or man, lets keep this equal.)

OMENS, CURSES & SUPERSTITIONS

■ Looking over another's shoulder into a mirror.

■ Coming in by one door and going out by another.

■ Meeting a cross-eyed person.

■ To cross knives on a table or to leave a knife turned blade upwards.

■ To have a lone Black crow fly over your head. (They always seem to zero in on my freshly washed car.)

■ To be called back just as you have begun a journey.

The Superstitious Theater

Jennie Grimard writes that actors are probably the most superstitious people around. Their careers, it is said, are in "the laps of the gods." If you are caught whistling in the dressing room, your fellow actors will condemn you, for you will "whistle up failure" for the show. Do not place a hat on a bed. Performers don't like this, especially in their dressing rooms.

It is advised never to look into a mirror over another person's shoulder because the person in front will be struck by a stroke of bad luck. Practicing before going on stage is essential, but never say the exact number of lines or it is certain you will forget some.

OMENS, CURSES & SUPERSTITIONS

The color yellow in a set or the color green in a costume is not used unless absolutely necessary. These colors are avoided since they were used to represent Satan in the Mystery Play. Having three candles lit in the dressing room or on stage is said to provoke quarrels and therefore is avoided.

Ironically, a black cat in the theater is considered good luck. The Haymarket Theater in London's West End had a black cat as a permanent resident. Saying "Good Luck" to another actor will bring them just the opposite. It is more appropriate to say "Break a Leg!" or "Merde!"

If you trip on your first entrance, don't be discouraged; it's a sign of good luck. To use a cane on stage is a sign of success, but crutches will bring failure. Knitting on stage is avoided since it will entangle the production.

Married actors find it very unlucky to remove their wedding rings while on stage. If it is truly unavoidable, they would have to cover it up with make-up or with masking tape. It is considered unlucky to allow someone not associated with the play to see you in costume before you go on stage.

If the show is a success on opening night, do not change your costume. If you change your costume the show will lose its appeal. At the end of a play's run, it is believed to be unlucky if you keep a costume or prop used in the play.

The most common theater superstitions are those revolving around Shakespeare's Macbeth. An actor will never quote any verse from "the Scottish play" before or after a show. It is said to be a truly evil play and that the song the three witches sing could really summon demons. If the dreaded word is uttered in the theater, you must immediately leave the theater, turn around three times, spit on the ground and then ask for permission to re-enter.

OMENS, CURSES & SUPERSTITIONS

Using An Egg To Remove Bad Luck

For many years the ancient Voodoo priests have used the power of eggs to help combat the power of evil spells and bad luck. They believe that the egg possesses strong magical powers and in the right hands can cause bad luck or good luck depending on the will of the practitioner. If you are plagued by evil spells and bad luck, try this powerful ancient Voodoo egg spell to help you remove any negative conditions from your life.

You must purchase a brown fresh egg before noon of that day. Make sure that you start this when the moon is waning. It is very important that this egg be fresh. Place this egg in a brown bag and tie the neck of the bag with a black cloth string. Place this bag under your bed.

Each night before retiring to bed, you must open this bag and take the egg out and rub it all over your body. When done, put the egg back into the bag, take a deep breath and blow three times into the bag. When you are blowing into the bag, you must imagine that all the bad luck is leaving your body, via your breath.

When done, place the bag back under your bed. Do this for nine days. At the end of nine days, take the bag with the egg and dispose of it outside your home. A good idea anyway, considering you've had the egg under your bed for nine days.

Each time that you blow into the bag, you must immediately tie it back up. If by the end of seven days you notice that your bag is moving on it's own. Stop, and dispose of the bag immediately. Do not look into the bag. Make sure that the bag is secure. Only do this if you are serious about destroying the bad luck in your life.

OMENS, CURSES & SUPERSTITIONS

Salt Lore

Food has always been of major importance to all people. Where food is concerned new superstitions are being born every year with every new diet that is published. Probably some of the oldest superstitions around concern salt. For salt was the one absolute pure substance as well as being the most common preservative, and no medieval home was without several bags of it.

Salt comes from Mother Earth, from the sea. Our tears and saliva taste of salt. Our blood, our very life consisted and depended on salt. "With all thine offerings thou shalt offer salt." (Leviticus 585 BC)

The Sky God, Ukko, cast a spark of fire which turned into salt, from the heavens into the sea, according to a Finnish myth. In the Old Testament, the eternal bond between God and Israel is depicted as a covenet of salt. (II Chronicles 13:5) For Christianity salt was an element of the holy water used in exorcism and in baptism.

In Homers *Iliad*, Patroclus scatters the embers and lays the spits above them after sprinkling the meat with holy salt for sacrifice to the gods. Probably the use of salt as a condiment and embellishment for food arose simply from this ritual. It helped to appease the gods and it tasted great too!

Brewers of Scotland put a handful of salt on top of the mash to ward off evil spirits.

Both Romans and Greeks worshiped a goddess of salt. They believed that salt purified the sea, and since their living came from the sea, they were at the mercy of these goddesses. During this time people would place a pinch of salt on a newborn's tongue to insure good health and long life.

OMENS, CURSES & SUPERSTITIONS

There is a superstition in Argentina that you don't pass around salt at the dinner table. You sit it down and let the next person pick it up.

The word salary pertains to salt because the Roman Empire paid soldiers with salt. From this we get the saying "He isn't worth his salt."

Also because of salt's preserving nature, Arabs along with many other nationalities still put salt into the coffin as a reminder of the soul's survival.

Pliny, the Elder (circa 77 A.D.) prescribed a grain of salt taken with a small amount of poison at a time to become immune to poison, and thereby avoid ever being poisoned. We accept an exaggeration with a grain of salt, as if we were trying to become immune to such overstatements.

It was believed that black magicians and necromancers were thought to never eat salt with their bread before raising the dead, as it would cancel out their spells. Similarly, alchemists held salt as symbolic of the body, the female, and earth. In their attempts to create gold, white salt was one of the ingredients often used.

A pinch of salt is often left in a baby's cradle to guard it against evil until baptized. Another tradition holds that a child's first tooth to come out should be placed in salt before it is cast into a fire.

It was thought unlucky to salt your own food, since salt symbolizes friendship, your fellow diner should do this for you. Wearing a small bag of salt around your neck is a surefire way to keep away the evil eye.

OMENS, CURSES & SUPERSTITIONS

Italian tradition says that when moving into a new house or apartment, have a new broom, a box of salt, and a loaf of bread on hand. While carrying the bread, you need to sprinkle the salt into the corners of one room, sweep it out of the room and out the outside door. Doing so insures that bad luck will be swept up with the salt and deposited outside.

Spilling Salt

All the way from ancient times until today, the spilling of salt is the most unlucky of accidents unless you quickly took a pinch and threw it over your left shoulder. "Right into the Devils face." It was believed that the devil would dance at our left side, just waiting to inflict all kinds of bad luck on us. Others say to avert bad luck when you spill salt, throw some of it over your right shoulder using the left hand. To avert bad luck when you spill salt, drop some of it into the fire or on the stove. Some say you must not speak between the spilling and the burning.

To avert bad luck when you spill salt, burn some of it while wishing the bad luck on an enemy. (You really shouldn't do this, any curse you send will bounce back to you three-fold. This is really bad Karma.)

If at the table you upset the saltcellar and the salt falls in your direction, you will have bad luck. If it falls towards someone else, good luck. The person who spills salt it is believed will be soon disappointed. This disappointment can be counteracted by throwing some of the salt over the left and then the right shoulder.

Whoever spills salt will soon be angry without reason. After you spill salt, you will have a quarrel. If you spill salt, you have an unknown enemy.(The person who has to clean it up afterwards.) If you spill salt, an enemy wants to become your friend.

OMENS, CURSES & SUPERSTITIONS

Unlucky Thirteen

Almost everyone knows about the alleged bad luck on Friday the thirteenth. From the most ancient times, the number thirteen was ill-fated, primarily because of the violent deaths of various ancient thirteenth gods, and of the fate of the thirteenth guest at Jesus' Last Supper. In case you didn't know it, the name for the fear of the number thirteen is: *Triskaidekaphobia*.

It is thought that thirteen people sitting at a table or meeting in a room means one of them will die before the year is out. For the ancient Egyptians, the number thirteen repersented the final step of a ladder of twelve that lead to eternal life. The Romans associated thirteen with death and misfortune.

The mathematician and mystic Pythagoras. who, in the sixth century BC, declared that the number twelve embodied perfection. By going twelve one better, Pythagoras implied, thirteen was unstable, imperfect, unlucky.

Some say that the Hindus created the idea of thirteen people at a table being unlucky. In Norse mythology, however, a story is told of an unlucky dinner to which twelve gods were invited. After everyone had arrived, Loki, the Norse God of Mischief, crashed the party as an uninvited guest. During this dinner, one of the gods was killed. What a way to ruin a perfectly good party!

Thirteen Floors?

Hotel management and architects usually avoid a thirteenth floor in their buildings. Even if there is an actual thirteenth floor, it is often numbered fourteen. Check this out for your self the next time you're in a high-rise building. More then likely the elevator buttons will be missing the thirteenth floor. There is also no Gate thirteen at National Airport in Washington D.C. Many airlines delete the thirteenth row of seats from their planes. In 1965, when Queen Elizabeth visited West Germany, her platform number at the Duisburg Railway station was changed from 13 to 12-A.

Thirteen at dinner is considered to be unlucky. The French avoid the problem by inviting quatorziemes, literally, fourteenths, to round up a guest list. The Savoy Hotel of London keeps a large wooden figure of a cat on hand, ready at a moment's notice to occupy the fourteenth chair.

One exception to the rule of unlucky thirteen is an office building in downtown Indianapolis, Indiana. Its address is 13 South Meridian street. It was opened on a Friday the thirteenth. The owners are so proud of their heritage that they have located their main offices on floor number thirteen. While some would think this was pushing luck a little too far, you might want to consider that the business has been open and successful for over fifty years.

In the United States, thirteen is really considered to be a lucky number. The Masonic symbol of the Great Seal of the United States, which appears on the back of the one dollar bill, contains a pyramid of thirteen steps. There are thirteen leaves and berries on the olive branch. The eagle, too, holds thirteen arrows in its claw. Of course lets not forget that the original colonies numbered thirteen.

One Aztec legend that has lingered since the ancient times tells of the thirteen life size skulls which were known as the Crystal Skulls of Wisdom. These ancient peoples used these gruesome artifacts to sing and speak as oracles. Four of these crystal skulls have now been found. The first was discovered in 1927 in the jungles of Belize by the British explorer Frederick Mitchell-Hedges. Nine more wait to be revealed. The legend states quite clearly that these 13 skulls will one day be reunited. When this happens they will foretell the destiny of humankind.

OMENS, CURSES & SUPERSTITIONS

Friday the Thirteenth

"Now Friday came, you old wives say. Of all the week's the unluckiest day." This short rhyme dates from the 17th century and even before that, in Chaucer's time (1300s), the worst day of the week was always held to be a Friday. The origin is Christian concerning the belief that Jesus died on a Friday.

The word Friday comes from the name **Freya**, the Teutonic Goddess of love. Although Friday is considered unlucky, it is generally considered good to be born on this day. Children born on a Friday are said to have the gift of curing fevers and will have numerous visions and second sight.

In the two different versions of the well-known rhyme describing the characteristics of someone born on each of the days of the week, "Fridays Child" is either "loving and giving" or "full of woe." The exception to the bad omens of Friday is Good Friday, which is, among other things, held to be the best day on which to wean children.

Tradition holds that Adam and Eve fell from grace on Friday, that the great flood was started on Friday, and that the temple of Solomon fell on Friday. Friday is considered an unlucky day on which to get married, to sail, to start a new job, to open a new play, to cut one's nails and to change your bed linen. However, it is said that your Friday night dreams, if talked about the next day, will come true.

The tradition that Friday the thirteenth is unlucky was augmented by a certain Captain Friday who unwisely, broke every rule in the superstitions lore book. Not only did he refuse to have a gold coin laid beneath the mast of his new ship, but he also refused to have the traditional red ribbon tied to the first nail in the building of it.

OMENS, CURSES & SUPERSTITIONS

Captain Friday also allowed the building of the ship to commence on a Friday. In fact, he insisted on it. The final insult was that he begun his maiden voyage in the ship on a Friday. Needless to say, Captain Friday and his ship were never seen again. I once heard that sailors were so superstitious that they believed no ship should be launched in a week with a Friday in it, or a month with a thirteenth.

Weather superstition holds that should it rain on Friday, it will be clear on Sunday, although, rain or shine, it is still believed to be a bad day for one to court another's favors. In Italy, tenants will never enter a new house on Friday. In both the United States and Great Britain tradition assigned this day for the hanging of criminals. That is why Friday is often referred to as "Hangman's Day."

Another tradition says that should one commit a theft on a Friday, it will be unsuccessful and will most likely lead to one's arrest. Likewise, one should never go to trial on Friday, for he is likely to lose. One who sings on Friday will cry by Sunday.

You must consider of course, that the idea of Friday as a day of ill fortune comes chiefly from Christian sources and not from other religions. For instance, among the Hindus, Friday is considered lucky for the making of friends and the wearing of new clothes.

Chapter Four:
CURSES, FOILED ONCE AGAIN -- YOU DON'T HAVE TO BE SPOOKED ANY MORE!

OMENS, CURSES & SUPERSTITIONS

What is a Curse?

In my line of work I see what the castings of curses, evil spells, hexes, and evil prayers does to people's lives. I see people who come to me with painful stories and shattered lives. I often think how unfortunate are the people who cast these maladies for whatever reason. They have no idea the pain and suffering they cause, nor do they realize the harm they are doing to their own souls in the process.

Anger is always at the bottom of these problems. When a man or a woman gets angry to the point of wanting to cast a curse on another person, often they fail to think through the results of their actions. Anger needs an outlet, but not in the form of casting an evil curse. Curses are words that are formed and made real to create "a problem" in the accursed person's life.

Words play a big role in all kinds of castings. Whatever the attitude was at the time the curse was made, either by the way the words are used in spoken or written form, it has power to do as much damage as needed to the unfortunate person being cursed.

When people perform curses, they have no idea that this creates in their life a "karma" of retribution. Hinduism says that karma is a woman who acts like a mother who protects her children by making the problem return to those who caused it. The old adage "that sooner, or later this too will catch up to the person who did the wrong" is a true statement. That is why it is better to find another way to solve, or adjust the problem that has come into anger or disappointment.

Shielding Yourself From Curses

A shield is a force field of energy that is used to completely encompass the physical or spiritual body. It's use is mainly to help keep out unwanted vibrations such as curses, negativity, overload of emotions drawn from other people, and energy leeches.

People who have strong empathic talents and have difficulty in keeping other people's emotion at bay find the shield most useful, especially if you have to go to a store, school or the hospital. You may not even have to enter the building to pick up the vibrations, often the vibrations can leak out of the building and impregnate the surrounding area.

A shield can take many forms, such as: egg shape where you are the center yoke, a two way mirror which encompasses the body completely, suit of armor, a ball of light or anything else for that matter. Just as long as your subconscious can perceive it as a protective force-field surrounding you.

The shield can be created in many different ways: ritual, visualization, and concentration. The actual creation of the shield can take many forms. Many people will place themselves in a small private pool of water with a waterfall. The water should be perceived as flowing energy. You then visualize the energy swirling around you, solidifying into a strong impregnable force field, allowing it to take on whatever form you choose. There are many different ways of drawing down the power, just choose one that feels compatible with you.

Do you want this shield to be temporary or on a more permanent basis? You don't have to set a real time date, but it helps to know if you need it just for a few hours or for several months. When you decide you don't need or want it anymore, you can terminate the shield.

To keep the shield going for a long term period you can do an up keep and maintenance of the shield by drawing more energy into the shield to replenish it. There will be times that your shield might weaken from daily use. The strain of daily pressures and stress can put the shield in a weakened condition. Also, being around large electromagnetic fields, such as large power plants and high voltage electric lines can cause tearing in the shield,.

All you have to do is recharge by drawing down more energy when you need it. You might have to discharge all the energy into the earth first, otherwise you might find yourself out of balance. Excess energy can cause you to feel jittery, nervous, tense, so ground yourself first and release the energy back into the earth. Then, when you have settled down, you can recharge yourself or make a new shield if necessary.

Avoiding The Evil Eye

Wynn Parks wrote in *The World and I* magazine that belief in the evil eye is widespread and ancient, and for those who believe themselves afflicted, the effects of the evil eye are not to be taken lightly. Throughout history people have believed that eyes have the power to beguile, leading to such wide spread sayings as "If looks could kill."

Because of universal and ancient belief in the evil eye, the symbol isn't likely to disappear from man's collective psyche soon. In Spain, 10,000-year-old cave drawings include magical symbols that are still used around the Mediterranean as protection against being "overlooked." In the northeastern United States, traces of evil eye belief can be found in the traditional hex designs painted on barns by the Pennsylvania Dutch.

Plato and the Pythagorean philosophers of Greece described "seeing" as a process in which emanations from the eyes encompassed the object. This understanding of vision as an active, quasi-spiritual illumination prevailed in Europe through the Middle Ages. The projected illumination could be good or evil, depending on the spiritual state of the beholder.

Those in love beamed forth grace. It was the envious glance that was to be guarded against. Envy, companion of Anger, Lust, Gluttony, and the rest of the seven deadly sins, whoever provoked Envy by his actions or appearance might find himself afflicted with the evil eye.

F.T. Elworthy, a nineteenth-century expert on evil eye folklore and author of a definitive work on the subject, perceived two forms of the evil eye: the moral and the natural. The two late-Victorian categories may be considered to correspond, roughly, to our contemporary distinctions of conscious and unconscious.

A "moral" evil eye occurs when a malicious individual consciously hexes another, as by witchcraft or sorcery. A "natural" evil eye is an affliction to its possessor, an unconscious trait, beyond the exercise of his will. One ancient story of a "natural" evil eye, found with variations from the eastern Mediterranean to Mexico, tells of an unfortunate father who is possessed of a natural evil eye and finally blinds himself to avoid afflicting his children.

For those who believe, the effects of the evil eye are not to be taken lightly. The victim feels jinxed, melancholy, and weak, or encounters an unprecedented run of bad luck or misfortune. Animals, children, and the elderly are most vulnerable, but even adults in good health have been stricken and even died, where extreme passion was involved behind the envious eyes.

Traditional wisdom on how to recognize a carrier of the evil eye varies. Aside from being wary of people with curious squints or strangely shaped pupils, the Mediterranean peoples historically have been suspicious of those with blue eyes. Northern Europeans have looked askance at dark eyes.

OMENS, CURSES & SUPERSTITIONS

Techniques to avert the evil eye generally fall into two categories: distracting the evil first glance, or negating its spiritual poison with counter magic. For distraction, one early Italian merchant had a decorative figure of a dwarf inset above the front door of his mansion. The gargoyle, grinning over its left shoulder while squatting with its pants crumpled around its ankles, presented all whose gaze fell on the house with the white-marble moon of its backside.

Because eye distractions must be visible to be effective, partially seen or even concealed amulets must possess magical potency. For Muslims, the holy color blue alone is held to be sovereign protection. It can be seen today in everything from the blue domes of mosques to the strings of blue beads that decorate animal harnesses. One of the most common charms seen hanging around the necks of men is the miniature shape of a horn. Its slight curve and pointed end make the horn a complex symbol invoking both phallic magic and the threat of a stabbing weapon.

Pre-Christian gemstones used as amulets were frequently engraved with a minute figure stabbing a huge eye. Being a double horn shape, the crescent moon is thought to have been, originally an appeal to Artemis, moon goddess and protectress of women and children from malign influences. Today, from Ireland to Turkey, carriage-horse harnesses are still decorated with protective silver crescents, while man-in-the-moon pendants swing from the necks of fashionable passengers.

Hand gestures in defense of the evil eye are also popular. The Greek uses an open-palm thrust, called a *moutza*, with which he mimes pushing excrement into the evil countenance. In Italy, a vulgar gesture called the *fica* is made by pushing the thumb between the first and middle fingers. From among such gestures we can deduce the evolution of what North Americans call the "bird."

OMENS, CURSES & SUPERSTITIONS

Cures For the Evil Eye

Even with an arsenal of defenses against being "overlooked," there are casualties. Most cures operate as if the evil eye victim has been charged with a malevolent energy. Anthropologists doing fieldwork in Mexico learn not to admire young children too enthusiastically, for this is one way to inflict the mal de ojo (evil eye). However, if such a mistake occurs, the redress is to touch the child, preferably on the head, drawing off the possibly harmful effect of over admiration.

For a bad case of the "eye," specialists called curanderos (healers) are sought out. A successful and benevolent curer may gain an almost saintly reputation, and the afflicted travel considerable distances for treatment. The curandero commonly begins with prayer. He often follows this with therapy known as curar con blanquillos, in which the preliminary procedure is to rub the nude patient all over with a fresh, white, unbroken egg. After a feverish patient is rubbed, the egg is submersed in a stream to dissipate the patient's heat. If an evil eye victim is rubbed, evidence that the malevolent influence has been drawn is seen when the egg is broken and its contents found to be curdling or even solidified as if hard-boiled.

In Turkey and other Mediterranean countries, the use of the blue bead has often been used for treatment against the evil eye. Aside from protecting its wearer from harm or evil, the blue bead is found often on rings and necklaces or among Turkish motifs. The blue bead is not only the most widespread talisman used to ward off evil in Anatolia, it is sometimes placed on silver or gold jewelry coupled with the inscription "God Bless."

It is also believed that the evil eye affects not only the humans, but it can also affect plants, animals, and homes so the blue bead is used to protect these as well. Another means of protection from the evil eye is prayer. Despite all types of talismans, a person who has been touched by the evil eye should be exorcised by a priestess or holy man.

OMENS, CURSES & SUPERSTITIONS

The Curse of The Kennedys

I think we are all more superstitious, more mystical, more religious then we care to admit. The most cursed family is a name often used in reference to the Kennedys. With the continuing heartbreak that haunts the Kennedys, it is as if some unseen and unforgiving force has built a house of misery for the Kennedys.

Cursed and star-crossed are terms used to describe the life and often tragic deaths of the Kennedys. "Of course, it is a death wish, born out of their solemn belief that they had the Divine Right of Kings." John Davis is a cousin to the late Jackie Kennedy Onassis, and a self-avowed "Kennedy-Watcher." He is a best-selling author and a man who grew up and flourished around Camelot.

"The Kennedys were always brought up to believe they were above the law. The tragic skiing death of Michael Kennedy on New Year's Eve had already been written by the fates. He had to do what he had to do. It was in the script. Reckless and why? Because the Kennedys can control life here in the United States. Nevertheless, they cannot control fate and life as it really is."

The late Joe Kennedy made his fortune on bootlegging during prohibition. Though Joe Kennedy's political career fizzled, he survived to put his son John in the White House at any cost. "Joe Kennedy was a rather well-dressed hoodlum," said John Davis, "smart beyond any standards, ruthless beyond any standards. He taught his family that winning isn't everything, but was the ONLY thing."

Unfortunately, the result of Joe Kennedy's life choices seems to have been passed down to the succeeding generations of Kennedys. Bad luck and misfortune seem to dog the family like the constant swarm of paparazzi who hover ever watchful for the first opportunity to strike.

OMENS, CURSES & SUPERSTITIONS

Michael Kennedy's death on a mountainside at age 39 is but the latest in what has been a decades-long roster of pain and anguish for the Kennedys, a list that includes ...1 World War II, another by a drug overdose ...1ded in acquittal.

...1 on a commitment to public service that has ...1nited States has had to a royal family, one ...1 them larger than life to ordinary Americans.

...y, more tragedy, more adversity," historian ...akespearean level. There is just an uncanny

...ath were almost universal in pointing out how ...d over the years. "I don't know anyone who ...y has had," Boston Mayor Thomas Menino ...ay for great glories."

The legacy of tragedy dates back to World War II, when Joseph P. Kennedy Jr., the eldest son of the Joseph and Rose Kennedy, was shot down over the English Channel and died at 29. Later came the assassination of President Kennedy in 1963 in Dallas. Five years after that, Robert F. Kennedy was shot and killed in Los Angeles moments after accepting victory in the California presidential primary. The following year, their brother the senator, Ted Kennedy drove his car off a narrow bridge on Chappaquiddick Island in Massachusetts. He survived, but his aide Mary Jo Kopechne was killed.

The 1980s and 1990s brought new problems to a new generation of Kennedys. Robert Kennedy's son David died of a drug overdose in 1984. William Kennedy Smith was charged with rape at the family home in Palm Beach, Fla., but was acquitted by a jury in 1991. Finally, with the accidental death of Michael Kennedy is a reminder that tragedy continues to stalk this privileged family.

JFK Jr.'s wife, Carolyn, was so shaken by Michael's skiing death that she is convinced a dark cloud hangs over the family. She fears something terrible will happen to John as well. Carolyn has bought her husband a gold St. Christopher's medal, and insists he wear it around his neck at all times.

Is the Kennedy family cursed? The Bible in *Exodus*, Chapter 20 says: "For I, the lord your God, am a jealous God, inflicting punishment for their father's wickedness, on the children of those who hate me, down to the third and fourth generation." Said John Davis: "I won't go into that, but it does demand some attention. After all, it is the Bible.

Papa Doc Duvalier, former dictator of Haiti is said to have cursed the Kennedy family for generations to come. It seems to have been a well laid curse.

Chapter Five:
TAILS OF THE BLACK DOG AND BAYING WOLVES

OMENS, CURSES & SUPERSTITIONS

Scratch a dog and you'll find a permanent job.
Franklin P. Jones

I've often wondered what the real meaning behind the old saying "Never look a gift horse in the mouth." There's got to be some sort of hidden meaning that has to do with a superstition. The obvious meaning is you can tell how old and what kind of health a horse is by checking out his teeth. So it wasn't good manners to look too closely if you were given a horse as a present. Then again, some horses I've known were rather ill tempered beasts. If you looked in their mouths you were sure to get a nasty nip.

So alright, I may not be the world's greatest expert on superstitions when it comes to horses, but hay -- no pun intended -- I do know a hell of alot about dogs and omens. For the most part, I've always figured howling dogs can be a good or bad sign, depending upon what side of the fence you are caught peering over.

According to superstition, the howling of a dog can be considered a negative sign. We know that dogs can sense trouble a mile away. Throughout history, there have been instances when doom has been associated with the restlessness of dogs. Signs and omens concerning howling dogs are even spoken about in Homer's *Odyssey*. The dogs of Eumaeus are described as terrified at the sight of Minerva, though she was invisible to human eyes. Read the book, I haven't read it since the time I lost it on a city bus.

In the old days, a howling dog was also an omen that someone in the village was about to die; today it probably means someone is trying to get in your basement, (could be "death" for them if they should meet up with my pups).

If you happen to look out the window and the weather doesn't look particularly inviting and your pet poodle starts to scratch at the screen door, (or your prize leather couch), chances are a bad storm is about to strike. If you were a bit prone to finding a "scientific" explanation this reaction may have something to do with the electrons in the air making the dog's hair stand on end; but after all this isn't a book on science, so forget about what I just said.

A Haunting We Will Go

We psychics all know that dogs are clairvoyant (why else would their ears perk up when a friend, or an intruder, is still down the block thinking about ringing your doorbell. Here's a little personal tid-bit that a friend of mine told me during a break in a reading I was doing for her.

The lady said she owned a black terrier named Sheba. When she gave birth to her son, Sheba became jealous of the boy and started snapping and growling as the child slept in its crib and later crawled around on the floor.

When the woman scolded the dog, the terrier growled at its owner in a most menacing way. My friend tried to give the dog away, but it had become so mean that nobody wanted to take it in. Eventually, the animal had to be put to sleep.

To this day, in quiet times, she can still hear the dog whimpering and howling at the door trying to get in. However, when the woman checks outside, there's no dog around. She says she is sure that it is Sheba, because she recognizes the dogs particular bark.

OMENS, CURSES & SUPERSTITIONS

Hair of The Dog

We've all heard the term "cut the hair of the dog that bit you." Today it can refer to the hangover cure of taking a drink when you first get up in the morning after a night of partying. Makes sense, you can avoid a hangover by never sobering up.

Superstitious lore loves the concept of "like cures like." Put another way, we believe that if something bad happens to us we will best cure the problem with more of the same. The belief is borne out by the medical principle of inoculation in which carefully measured doses of a virus are injected into the body in order to build up an immunity against the disease.

The original source of the superstition came about from a story of a man who was bitten by a dog. He grabbed the animal, cut its hair and used the hair to stop the flow of blood. He kept the hair thereafter in the belief that it would provide healing abilities for any wound he or anyone else might sustain.

Other Doggy Superstitions

A dog passing between a couple about to be married means ill fortune will befall the couple. A dog digging a large hole in your garden means there will be a death in the family. Being followed by a strange dog indicates good luck.

Measles can be cured by placing a hair from the patient's head between two pieces of buttered bread and giving it to a dog. You can also determine if an sick person will recover by rubbing his teeth with a piece of food and throwing it to a dog. If the dog eats it, it is a good sign. If the dog turns up his nose, the sick person could die.

OMENS, CURSES & SUPERSTITIONS

If a dog falls asleep with his paws drawn up around him and his tail outstretched, in some parts of the world it is said to indicate a death. The direction of the death can be determined by which way the animal's tail is pointing.

The Irish believe that it is unlucky to meet a barking dog first thing in the morning. According to the Chinese, a dog has seven consecutive lives. The Moslems say a dog must not be killed, since its life equals that of seven men. The Normans said all dogs belong to Satan, except sheep dogs.

If a dog passes between two friends, it will mean an end to the friendship. If a dog runs between the legs of a woman, her father or husband will soon be punishing her. If a dog is seen eating grass, rolling on the ground, or scratching itself for a long time, it means that it will soon rain.

Dogs are thought to be able to see evil spirits and will warn their owners of their presence. It is considered sacrilege for a dog to enter a church. In many country parishes in Britain, a "dog whipper" was employed to expel any dogs that might enter the church during a service.

Tails of the Black Dog

Perhaps the custom of the "dog whipper" was not such a bad idea. Stories of demonic black dogs associated with churches have been told and retold over the years. Janet and Colin Bord in their book *Alien Animals* (Stackpole Books, 1981), relates an interesting story of a church invading black dog.

On Sunday, August 4, 1577 in the Bungay church in Suffolk England, a terrible storm arose and a black dog suddenly appeared. His presence was fatal, for when he passed between two members of the congregation: "as they were kneeling upon their knees, and occupied in prayer as it seemed, wrung the necks of them both at one instant clean backward, insomuch that even at a moment where they kneeled, they strangely died."

Another man was injured when the black dog : "gave him such a gripe on the back, that therewith all he was presently drawn together and shrunk up, as it were a piece of leather scorched in a hot fire; or as the month of a purse drawn together with a string. The man, albeit he was in so strange a taking, died not, but as it is thought is yet alive."

Abraham Fleming, who reported this event in *A Straunge and Terrible Wunder*, also told of a similar event that occurred the same day in the nearby Blythburgh church.

"On the self-same day, in like manner, into the parish church of another town called Blibery, not above seven miles distant from Bungay above said, the like thing entred, in the same shape and similitude, where placing himself upon a main balke or beam, whereon some ye Rood did stand , suddenly he gave a swing down through ye church, and there also, as before, slew two men and a lad, and burned the hand of another person that was there among the rest of the company, of whom divers were blasted. This mischief thus wrought, he flew with wonderful force to no little fear of the assembly, out of the church in a hideous and hellish likeness."

This is apparently not the only occasion when a large dog has been seen inside a church in frightening circumstances. A twelfth century French historian named Bertin wrote in his pamphlet called *Annales Francorum Regum*, that in 856 AD, a storm arose at Trier during a service. The church was "filled with such dense darkness that one and another could hardly see or recognize his or her neighbor. On a sudden, there was seen a dog of immense size in a sudden opening of the floor or earth, and it ran to and fro around the alter."

OMENS, CURSES & SUPERSTITIONS

Again at Trier, a large dog was seen in the pontifical chair of the great church in 867AD. According to *Chronicon Saxonicus,* "a certain priest at midnight, in the presence of the whole congregation, was cast down by lightning, with no other injuries, but what looked like a pig or black dog was seen to run to and fro between his feet." The priest died from his injuries. However, no animals were found in the church, the congregation felt that they had been cursed by the devil, and many never returned to that particular church.

A Tudor historian, John Stowe, wrote of a visitation suffered by St. Michael's church, Cornhill, London. "There arose a tempest of thunder and lightning, and a thing of an ugly shape and sight was seen to come in at the south window." The black dog reportedly left deep claw marks on stones in one of the church windows."

The black dog has its roots buried deep in folklore. It is an enigmatic creature, friendly in some places, an omen of death or disaster in others. Whatever the significance of the encounter, people who have seen the strange animals are unlikely to forget the experience. The black dog is generally thought of as peculiarly British, however, there are accounts of black dogs from Ireland, France, Italy, Croatia, Germany, Austria, Poland, and the United States and Canada.

In traditional superstition, seeing a black dog indicates bad weather is on the way. It is interesting to note the stories of the black dogs that wrecked such havoc in Bungay and Blythburgh churches in 1577, did so during a terrible storm. Which came first? The superstition that seeing a black dog means a coming storm. Or the black dog incidents which later caused the storm superstition to be told?

Not all black dog superstitions are bad. It is believed that the black dog can be a guardian that protects men, women, and children. There are tales of mysterious black dogs protecting lonely travelers against robbers, and on the Isle of Man there was a black dog which prevented a fishing crew from sailing to their possible deaths when a gale was imminent. The black dog is also widely known as a treasure guardian throughout northern Europe.

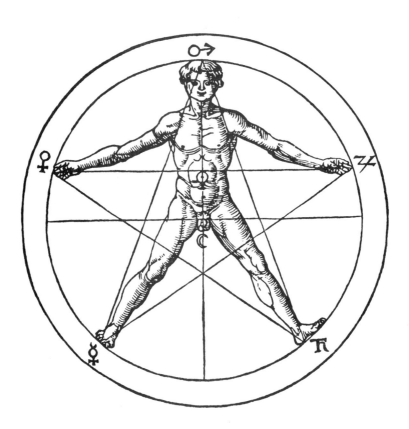

Chapter Six:
BIRDS,
BLACK CATS AND
OTHER ANIMAL OMENS

OMENS, CURSES & SUPERSTITIONS

The development of animals in mythology and folklore has seen a variety of creatures with the abilities of speech, and what are now known as PSI, psychokinesis (PK) telepathy and clairvoyance. This was believed to indicate that nature itself was attempting to communicate with Man with the aim of raising the consciousness to influence his spiritual and physical being.

Sometimes the message bearing animal appeared at a particularly crucial time so that the advice given was perceived as positive and generally agreeing with the instinctual nature in man. Ignoring the advice given often led to bad luck. Eventually though, the ability of man to understand what was being said resulted in a positive outcome or reward. Talking animals were also seen as mediators, and were sometimes shown as contrasting forces, for example the lion and the unicorn which demonstrated the juxtaposed physical and spiritual qualities to be pursued.

Composite animals, such as mermaids, were often seen as symbolic of the inner struggles of man with his culture together with his environment. Bigfoot has been said to indicate, in many of the legends, a symbolic need for man to be civilized within mythology and life itself, with animal instincts to be driven out and replaced with moral codes of behavior.

The actions of mythological and folkloric animals have been attributed as information giving, or in some cases were seen to be omen indicators. These omens were allied to the idea of warnings indicating perhaps events to come but not causing the event itself. The omen could indicate an immediate, short or long term outcome depending on the animal concerned.

Man could then take precautions and use his wisdom as developed through understanding of the folklore instruction. Omens were traditionally connected with dreams and oracles, believed to be physical messages from other worlds to be heeded. The codes of practice set-up were ritualized and practiced by whole communities with each person playing a part for the improvement of the whole. Some animals were used to demonstrate the conflict and harmony between man and woman. Sometimes the feminine qualities within a man were explored through superstition and myth, as a sense of sexuality today is explored.

The powers of darker forces within the world's religions have come to be seen to dominate all folklore, with the eternal desire and search for justice and enlightenment. The sense of a people and a community can be gleamed from the rituals associated with protection or reverence discussed within the superstition. The consequences of ignoring advice were shown within each story. From these superstitions, the patterns of life could be formed to provide a communal stability in all aspects of life.

Cats to be Feared - Cats as our Friends

Throughout ancient cultures feline deities have been protective forces. Sekmet and Bast are Egyptian cat deities. Sekmet rules over the destiny of humanity as the "Goddess of Fate." She is a fiery solar goddess. While Bast is protective in a more joyous way.

Bast is known as the Mother of all Cats and their protector. In Egypt, the punishment for killing a cat was death. Thousands of cats were mummified at death and buried with cat statues and other items they would need in the afterlife. In Egypt it was believed that a black cat crossing one's path brought good luck.

Cats are well known as familiars of witches. During the burning times, thousands of cats were burned along with accused witches, healers, and wisewomen. Today, most black cats will have a spot of white on them because practically all pure black cats were killed during past witch hunts.

OMENS, CURSES & SUPERSTITIONS

In ancient Atlantis, it is said that priests used cats as spy tools. The priest class could not use crystals when they traveled to other societies, as they were viewed as magic and feared. So they used cats as disguised amplification devices. They called them Ki-Tones (translated to harmonics). Later shortened to Keyt, then Kat, and then Cat.

A Norse legend tells of the chariot of Freya, the witch, that was pulled by black cats that became black horses. They were exceedingly swift and surely possessed by the Devil. After serving Freya for seven years, the cats were rewarded by being turned into witches, disguised as black cats. This seems to have led to the belief in the Middle Ages that black cats were familiars of witches, and after seven years, became witches themselves. They believed if a black cat crossed your path, Satan was taking notice of you.

The idolized cats of Egypt and the witch cats of Europe leave this superstition open to individual interpretation, so when a black cat crosses your path, take your pick.

- It is said that the tail of a black cat when placed on various parts of the body can induce healing.

- The skin of a black cat was believed to cure bad backs.

- If you place the bone of a black cat in your mouth, it will confer the power of invisibility.

- Cats are great at predicting the weather. When the cat is wild and playful, expect wind. When cats cozy up to the fire, expect a hard frost or snow. If you see a cat looking out the window, expect guests soon.

OMENS, CURSES & SUPERSTITIONS

- In Japan, cats are an ill-omen allegedly capable of killing women and assuming their appearance.

- In the Buddhist world, cats and snakes are blamed for being the only creatures unmoved by Buddha's death.

- The cat was a good omen in ancient China. Its gait was copied in rustic dances.

In Cambodia, a cat is carried around in a cage from house to house with songs and processions to pray for rain. The villagers pour water on the cat to awaken Indra with its howls. Indra is the giver of rain showers. So in essence, they associate the cat with droughts.

Islamic tradition views the cat favorably unless it is black. A completely black cat has magical properties; its flesh cures the bewitched. A black cats spleen will stop hemorrhages. Its blood is used to write powerful charms. It was thought that Jinns (genies), often appeared as a cat. So you should treat them politely when they enter your room at night.

In Sumatra, the Nias believe that the dead cross a bridge to get to heaven. Below them is the abyss of hell. A guard stands at the gate with a shield, a lance, and a cat to help him throw the sinners into the waters of hell.

To the Pawnee Indians of North America, the evil cat is symbolic of cunning, forethought, and ingenuity. It is a sacred animal who can only be killed for a ritual with religious purposes. Other than that, you were to leave cats alone.

OMENS, CURSES & SUPERSTITIONS

In central Africa, medicine bags are made with cat skins to aid in clairvoyance.

A strange black cat on your porch brings prosperity - *Scottish superstition.*

When you see a one-eyed cat, spit on your thumb, stamp it in the palm of your hand, and make a wish. The wish will come true - *American superstition.*

English schoolchildren believe seeing a white cat on the way to school is sure to bring trouble. To avert bad luck, they must either spit, or turn around completely and make the sign of the cross.

Cats purring is very healing. If you notice, they like to arrange themselves alone your chakras when you are resting, thereby healing and resonating with their owners.

When you are gifted with a cat, whether you think you choose the cat, or more then likely, the cat chooses you, consider yourself blessed. Let the cat help build a bridge between the earth plane and the spirit world. The cat will help you in your daily meditations and magical pursuits.

While the cat generally is respected, revered, and yes, maybe feared, the rabbit, however, has not been so lucky. A left hind foot, carried in the left pocket after having been removed from a rabbit that was killed during a full moon by a cross-eyed person is truly lucky. The foot is considered a powerful charm against evil because the rabbit's strong hind legs touch the ground before its front legs. Ancient people thought this so remarkable that they ascribed magical powers to it.

Since rabbits and hares are born with eyes open, which is an erroneous notion, they supposedly had special powers over the evil eye.

Because of the rabbit's ability to reproduce, the rabbit's foot also became a symbol of fertility.

The next time you see a full moon, look for the rabbit in the moon. Many cultures, including several Native American tribes, have legends about the markings on the moons surface that seem to form the shape of a rabbit.

Birds of a Feather

Out of all the animals, birds have probably elicited the most attention from humanity in the form of legends, myths, and superstitions. This sense of wonderment possibly came about because birds had accomplished the one thing that early man had dreamt of doing, but was unable, the ability to fly into the heavens.

It seems that birds naturally know certain things regarding future occurrences of the seasons, according to *Jeremiah 8:7*, "The kite in the air hath known her time; the turtle, the swallow, and the stork have observed the time of their coming." It was believed that natural knowledge was infallible and comes from God. From this belief came the use of the birds' knowledge in order to predict the future, and this was called divination by augury.

There is a story of a Zen Master who was beginning a lecture to his pupils and before he started a little bird flew in the window and started chirping. He stretched out his hand to his pupils for silence and the bird just sang up a wonderful tune. After awhile the bird flew off. The Zen master looked at his pupils and said "That was the sermon for the day. Class dismissed."

In ancient Celtic superstitions birds are usually used to represent prophetic knowledge, bloodshed, and skill. In an omen, birds can be either the message or the messenger. The interpretation of their calls and movements can lead to knowledge of future events. Birds, especially ravens and crows, usually presage bloodshed and battle. The Irish war goddesses were said to call the ravens down to battle fields to feast on the flesh of the slain. Even normal, modern crows and ravens descend to feed on corpses along the road.

Ravens are blackbirds, cousins to the crow. These birds of shining purple tinged wings and all-seeing black eyes have long been thought of as omens to humankind. It was a raven who was the first bird released from Noah's ark in the inundation that took so many of the Nephillim. The Raven abandoned Noah, preferring to fly above the waters alone rather than go back to the ark.

In the myths of the Norsemen, Odin-All Father, kept two oracular ravens named Hugin (Thought) and Munin (Memory) who kept him informed of all that went on in the world with their whispers. The Muslims call the raven Abu Zajir, which means the Father of Omens.

The Elizabethan writer, Christopher Marlow, who also wrote, *The Tragical History of Doctor Faustus*, wrote in his play, *The Jew of Malta*, this passage describing a raven: "Like the sad-presaging raven that tolls the sick man's passport in her hollow beak. And in the shadow of the silent night Doth shake contagion from her sable wing."

The raven is known throughout history as both portent and prophet. Among the Irish the term "Raven's Knowledge" is used when describing seers. These people with extra senses and often some ability to prophesy are compared to this bird to which man has attributed supernatural abilities.

In Brittany, birds were believed to answer questions with their song. Should the sound of the night jar be heard by a householder, death is likely. According to the Scots should a caged bird die on the wedding morning of a family member, the marriage will be unhappy and the couple will eventually separate.

British traditions hold that should a bird drop on you, it is considered bad luck. The Irish say that if black and gray birds are seen flying around trees in the dark, never settling, these are souls accomplishing penance.

Rural United States folklore says that if a hen starts to crow then bad luck is not far away. A storm is approaching when chickens run about flapping their wings.

Different birds can mean different things. Each species has their own rich mythology surrounding them. Over the years those who have studied birds and their habits have passed down the traditions associated with birds. Such books as: *Animal Speak*, by Ted Andrews, and, *Shamanic Wisdom II*, by Dolfyn and Swimming Wolf, list some known beliefs about the symbolic and portent meaning to certain birds.

Hawks: These birds represent nobility, recollection, cleansing, and illumination. The Egyptian God Horus was represented by a hawk.

Doves: Are associated with love, monogamous relationships, dedicated parenting. Invoke the dove for romance, love and loyalty. Bird of peace, prosperity, purity and spirit. Native Americans believed that mourning doves were lovers who had passed away leaving their true love behind. Their sad songs are meant for their lost loves to hear and rejoin them. The Greeks associated doves with Aphrodite, Goddess of love.

Eagles: Feathers are important healing tools for Native American shamans. Eagles symbolize courage, endurance, and fortitude. Eagles help us see clearly to develop our spiritual abilities. Many cultures see eagles as the Thunderbird which was associated with powerful storms. Invoke the eagle for clarity of vision, illumination, far reaching sight, and transcendence.

Hummingbird: This bird helps to move in new directions. Her energy assists with love, grace, beauty, delicacy, strength, and passion. The hummingbird also raises our vibration to endure the emotional and passionate conflicts associated with love. If you see a hummingbird, it is good luck.

Owl: Associated with wisdom and the darkness. The owl has the ability to move through the unknown. Use the owl symbol as an amulet against the Evil Eye. You may see an owl when a loved one is about to pass on. In Israel, grey owls near the crops were considered a good omen. Owls are symbolic of occult and psychic powers. Some alleged UFO abductees say that the Greys often put mental images of owls in the minds of the abductees. Owls are also thought of as a sign of upcoming change.

Peacocks: Provide psychic protection, especially against the Evil Eye. It is thought that if you keep peacock feathers in your house, they will protect you from the Evil Eye. Seeing peacocks is a sign of good luck and serenity.

Penguin: These birds represent lucid dreaming and astral projections. Dreaming of a penguin lets you know you need to adapt to your environment.

OMENS, CURSES & SUPERSTITIONS

Blackbirds: In general are associated with omens and mysticism. However, when blackbirds come into your life, you will open to new surprises and new understanding of natural forces.

Blue Jays: Teach us to be balanced in between the darkness and the light. Blue jays teach us that power is accessible from more than one place. Seeing blue jays shows you have a chance to move forward if you use your head.

Magpies: If you see magpies be sure to count them. Their number is significant. An old Scottish fortune telling rhyme states: "One's sorrow, two's mirth, three's a wedding, four's a birth, five's a christening, six a death, seven's heaven, eight is hell, and nine's the devil." Magpies are associated with witches and magicians. They can teach us to use our occult knowledge in a beneficial and appropriate way.

Vultures: Vultures are purifiers who assist us in cycles of death and rebirth.

Whippoorwill: The wailing of a whippoorwill portends death. The person who hears a whippoorwill calling at midnight will soon hear of a death.

The Coming of the White Buffalo

In the September 1996 issue of ***Share International Magazine***, Bette Stockbauer wrote about the birth of a white buffalo calf, considered to be a good omen for many Native Americans. In 1933 a white buffalo calf was born in Colorado, and in 1994 another one, named Miracle, was born in Janesville, Wisconsin, on the ranch of Dave and Valerie Heider.

OMENS, CURSES & SUPERSTITIONS

Thousands of people of many different faiths have visited Miracle, testifying that her birth is a call for all races to come together to heal the earth and solve our mutual problems.   On May 9 1996, a silvery-white buffalo calf named Medicine Wheel was born at the ranch of Joe Merrival on the Pine Ridge reservation of South Dakota. Another white calf, Rainbow, had been born in the same herd on 27 April. Unfortunately, it died 25 hours later of scours, a diarrhea-type condition.

The birth of a white buffalo calf is seen by the Native Americans as the most significant of prophetic signs, equivalent to the weeping statues, bleeding icons, and crosses of light that are prevalent within the Christian mythos. Just as the Christian faithful who attend these signs see them as a renewal of God's ongoing relationship with humanity, so do the Native Americans who see the white buffalo calf as a sign that humanity is running out of the time it has to cleanse or heal themselves.

The recent births were surrounded by controversy. Some have suggested that the calf is a beefalo, a buffalo and beef cattle mix. Some have accused Mr Merrival of genetic engineering. The odds of the birth of a white buffalo are estimated as 6-10 million to one. In response, he says that there is little probability of mixed parentage and none whatsoever of genetic manipulation.

Mr Merrival, who is of Oglala Sioux ancestry, thinks the birth of Medicine Wheel is a great gift that must now be used to try and help as many people as possible. His son Darrin, thinks that the calf was sent to us to unify the nation.

James Dubray, a medicine man, said: "Our young people need it the most. They need to have hope. They need to have a future. And this will help. This place has been chosen as the starting point for the healing process to begin."

Floyd Hand Looks For Buffalo, an Oglala medicine man, has commented: "Here is a man, a poor farmer, who has been kind to animals all his life, and now there is a white buffalo calf here. These are omens, and they are happening in the most unexpected place among the poorest people in the country. They are good omens, if we pay attention to them. For us, this would be something like coming to see Jesus lying in the manger."

When asked whether the birth of the latest calf was a sign, Benjamin Creme replied: "Yes indeed, it is a sign. The important ones are the last two. These were created with the influence of the Masters." As a result of these white buffalo's being born, Native Americans have greatly increased the frequency of ceremonies to bring back balance to the Earth before it is too late.

Animal Omens

Whatever you are doing, drop it if a weasel crosses your path: this dreadful beast brings signs of bad fortune.

If you hear an owl hooting in the forest before midnight, it warns of trouble to come. If heard after midnight, it is a sign that death is near.

When you see a frog in early spring, creep up behind it and gently stroke its back with your finger. You will know true love before the snow flies. (Probably the frog, they just love to be stroked.)

If you see a spider: In the morning-You'll know shame. At midday-pleasure and profit. In afternoon-a gift it brings. In the evening - joy and mirth.

OMENS, CURSES & SUPERSTITIONS

A spider found crawling on a person is good luck. "If you wish to thrive, Leave the spider alive." Only a spider killed in the house or one found on your person causes bad luck say some. The killing of a black spider or a baby spider is very unlucky.

Cattle should be weaned during the decline of the moon.

Give whiskey to an animal and its growth will stop. (I wouldn't suggest doing this, I don't want to be accused of contributing to the delinquency of an animal.)

Go to the cow shed on New Year's Eve at midnight and you will find the cows on their knees.

If you don't want your cattle in the barn to be sick, take a file and make three crosses on the doorsill they walk under.

Never enter a barn during a storm because cattle draw lightning.

Spit over you finger when you see a dead animal to prevent having bad luck.

Talk to your livestock at midnight on New Year's Eve and they understand you.

The only time to castrate an animal is during the sign of Scorpio, otherwise the animal will die.

Upon seeing crows, remember - One for sorrow, two for mirth, three for a wedding,

OMENS, CURSES & SUPERSTITIONS

four for a birth.

Bad tidings in one quarter; an omen of disaster in another yet all should know: Black cat arrives, good fortune thrives.

If this is your idea of a good time then the following is an old Celtic charm which will make the caterpillar worm destroy itself by twisting itself up to nothing:

Underneath this hazelen mot, there's a braggaty worm, with a speckled throat. Now! nine double hath he. Now from this nine double, eight double. From eight double, to seven double. From seven double, to six double. From six double, to five double. From five double, to four double. From four double, to three double. From three double, to two double. From two double, to one double. Now! No double hath he.

This charm, like all charms, must be muttered because they loose potency if uttered aloud, and the charmer may never communicate the charm to one of the same sex, for to do so would transfer the power of the charming to the other. I think this is an awful lot of trouble to kill a poor little caterpillar. That is of course as long as they are not infesting my garden, then its every caterpillar for themselves.

When the head of a household dies, someone must go and inform the bees, otherwise they will leave or die. This widely-held European belief stipulates that the bees were the messengers to the gods, and must be sent to inform them of the recent death. On the occasion of a death, the old people made it a point to drape the flowers with mourning and tell the news to the bees.

Mrs. Pascoe of St. Hilary in Great Britain, related in her memoirs that in 1838 she saw a bit of black flag attached to a churchwoman's flowers. She explained that since her son had died being burnt to death, the flowers had begun to wither away and were only revived after she put on the piece of mourning. A man in 1888 mentioned that as a boy he had seen thirty beehives belonging to Mr. Joshua Fox of Tregedna tied up in crepe because of a death in the family.

Another man at the same time said that recently he saw at the First and Last Inn in Land's End, at the death of its landlady, all of the flowers and birdcages creped in order to prevent their deaths.

Never kill a robin, bad luck will follow. Do not kill a swallow; it will make you unlucky. The killing of a wren is unlucky. Bad luck comes to those who kill a woodpecker. (Sounds like the birds have a strong union).

In Africa it is believed that If you see a chameleon walking head-first down a stick, or if you find one half buried, beware. This can cause a thin person to become stocky and vice versa. This is not a dietary tip; the weight shift is extreme enough to cause illness and death! Use as directed. If a chameleon is seen digging a hole, a relative will die. If you find a chameleon while plowing a field, it will greatly slow your progress.

If a snake is killed during the mating season, its mate will come to the body; before sunset say some, before noon next day say others. Never pick up a skin cast by a snake in early spring; you would be picking up a lot of trouble. The snake-doctor (dragon fly), warns a snake when danger is near.

Cures for Snakebite

Split open a black hen and bind it warm to the bitten place. If the flesh of the fowl darkens the poison has been drained from the bite; if not, the victim has absorbed the poison. Apply soda and lye soap to the bite. Suck the poison from the bite. This must be done by a person with red gums who has chewed a piece of tobacco before starting.

Kill the snake and tie it around the victim's foot. Dig a hole and bury the bitten foot. (I imagine you leave the foot attached to the leg. I don't know how long you have to stand around with your foot buried in a muddy hole.)

Mark Twain wrote about an old southern snakebite cure in *The Adventures of Huckleberry Finn*.

"Internally, give the patient all the Whisky he can drink. From a quart to a gallon should be drunk in six or eight hours. No fears need be entertained of making the patient drunk. You may fill him with Whisky, then let him swim in it, and it will not make him drunk, so long as the poison of the snake remains in the system....It is a complete antidote for Snakebite, if taken freely, and may be relied on in any and all cases. It should be drunk like water for a few hours, and continued, at short intervals, until the patient gives signs of intoxication, when the quantity should gradually be diminished as the disease is beginning to recede. Keep him 'under the influence of liquor,' however, until you are sure he is out of danger."

Chapter Seven:
DON'T FEAR THE REAPER -- LIVING WITH THE DEAD

OMENS, CURSES & SUPERSTITIONS

Then away out in the woods I heard that kind of a sound that a ghost makes when it wants to tell about something that's on its mind and can't make itself understood, and so can't rest easy in its grave and has to go about that way every night grieving.

Huck Finn

There are so many beliefs and traditions surrounding death that it is hard to know where to start. The dark angel of death, or the "grim reaper," brings many different manifestations in popular culture such as the dreaded shudder which indicates that someone is walking over our grave.

The factor that brings the rituals and rites surrounding death into the light, however, is the concept that it is not an ending but a beginning, and the final passage from life is yet only another rather than the last.

In ancient Egypt, pagan Europe, and old America, the rituals that surrounded burial make it perfectly clear that mankind understood there was to be a journey which was undertaken after the living human has "passed away." We still use this same term to describe the dead today, and the way in which burial chambers and graves were stocked with food, tools, and various other items indicates that the original concept of a continued existence of some kind was the most powerful of forces to create lore, a lore that we still give the greatest attention to.

A friend of mine remembers a ritual during car rides when we passed by a cemetery, we had to touch the car ceiling with both hands and lift our feet off the floor, or something bad would happen. What was the "something bad"? I never found out. I still hold my breath when driving by a cemetery to keep from breathing in any disembodied spirits. I've done this all my life.

OMENS, CURSES & SUPERSTITIONS

Here are some well-known, and some not- so-well-known omens about death.

- If a black beetle crawls up your sleeve.

- If a picture suddenly falls from the wall.

- If a cow moos after midnight.

- If you hear an owl outside your window seven days in a row.

- If a stopped clock suddenly begins to strike.

- If a bird flies into the house and sits on a bed.

- If a bird pecks at the side of a house.

- If a very ill person "picks at the bed covers."

- If you kill a redbird or a bluebird.

- If a rooster crows in the doorway, or a hen crows.

OMENS, CURSES & SUPERSTITIONS

- If you dream of a cemetery.

- If you hear 3 knocks on a door & no one's there. (signifies the sound of nails closing a coffin.)

- A window blind falling without any apparent cause.

- When 'rigor mortis' does not appear in a corpse it means that another family member will die soon.

- To dream of a wedding is a sure sign of a funeral.

- If a dead person's eyes are left open, he'll find someone to take with him.

- If a woman is buried in black, she will return to haunt the family.

- Mirrors in a house with a corpse should be covered or the person who sees himself will die next.

- The soul of a dying person can't escape the body and go to heaven if any locks are locked in the house.

- You will have bad luck if you do not stop the clock in the room where someone dies.

OMENS, CURSES & SUPERSTITIONS

Foretelling When Death Will Come A Knocking

It is believed that breaking a mirror will cause seven years of bad luck. This belief might have come from the superstition that if people would look into water, they could see their fates. If the image was distorted it was a sure sign of the viewer's death. Early people gazed into a mirror in the same way that someone might gaze into a crystal ball. He imagined he saw the image of his soul, which could detach itself from the body and actually be in the mirror. If the mirror was shattered so was the soul, and the person would die.

To find out when the grim reaper will come knocking on your door: On New Year's Eve at midnight, go into a dark room and look in the mirror. If you see a coffin, you will die within the next year.

Another method is to skip rope while singing this jump rope song:

> Apples, peaches, pumpkin pie
> How many years before I die
> One year, two years, three, four. . .
>
> (Jump rope until you miss!)

An ancient Jewish tradition says that it is possible for a husband and wife to learn who will die first by calculating the numeric value of the letters in each of their names: A=1, B=2, etc. Should the sum be even, the man is said to die first; if odd the women.

OMENS, CURSES & SUPERSTITIONS

In Brittany, on New Year's Day, fathers toss slices of buttered bread into the air, while naming family members one by one. Those slices that fall on the buttered side indicate those who will die in the year to come. (Doesn't bread always fall butter side down?)

Should one write the names of the wise men on his forehead with his own blood on the night of Epiphany and should he then look in the mirror, his own death time and circumstances will be seen.

The Welch believed that if a mole is found that has burrowed under the wash house or dairy, it is said that the woman of the house will die during the next year.

Once death has occurred, then the living are left with what remains, the corpse. The remains were subject to numerous requirements in the ancient lore and sources of superstitions. The corpse, when removed from the death bed, whether it be at home or from the hospital, must be carried out feet first. The human being comes into life head first and must therefore leave the other way.

Corpses aboard ships are considered very unlucky and must therefore be buried at sea as quickly as possible, again, dropping into the sea feet first, or they will bring either bad weather or bad fortune. Many a disaster at sea has been confirmed by the previous death of a member of the crew.

Never speak ill of the dead, but always utter phrases such as "poor man" or "honest man" or "rest his soul," otherwise the soul may come visiting, and boy will they be mad.

OMENS, CURSES & SUPERSTITIONS

Drownings

You will always find the body of a drowned woman floating face up; the body of a drowned man, face down.

To locate a drowned person, lay some quicksilver on the middle of a slice of bread and let the bread rest on the water where the person went down. The bread and quicksilver will float and stop above the submerged body.

As a last resort in recovering the body of a person who has drowned, set off a charge of dynamite in the water where the person sank. It is thought the explosion will cause the bladder to burst and thus raise the cadaver.

Ghosts

It was believed that when a person died, if his or her soul was somehow troubled, if it had been wronged in life or in its death, for example, or if the body were left unburied - it would roam a middle ground between the states of existence.

The souls of those dying violent deaths will wander the earth until released. The soul of a murder victim is said to remain on earth until the guilty person is found or until he himself is buried wearing the shoes that he wore at the time of the crime. Hanged persons were said to remain suspended between heaven and hell indefinitely.

It is frequently believed that if a mother dies in childbirth, she will remain behind in spirit form to make sure her child is safe. In parts of pagan Europe, if a mother died in childbirth and the child survived, the baby would be buried with the mother to make sure that she did not return in search of her child.

In China, there is a belief that the dead come back once a year on the last night of the year. A bed, food, and water are prepared for them, and a door is left open for them to enter.

Mark Twain's *America Bernard DeVoto* describes ghosts or "ha'nts" as follows: "The spirit left the corpse and entered a dreary state, less than life, not quite extinction. Such half-creatures flitted endlessly about the world, their passage marked by a small rustling or a tiny beat of wings. ... But for their envy, they would have had pathos."

Sudden Silence - It Must Be Twenty After

The most popular superstition on this subject, however, is the belief that when, for no apparent cause, everyone in a group suddenly seems at a loss for something to say, it must be twenty minutes after the hour. This idea is generally accepted by superstitious Americans, and is purely American in origin, going back to a legend which has grown around Abraham Lincoln's death.

For those who believe that the Great Emancipator died at 8:20 o'clock, a sudden silence is supposed to occur automatically ever since, through some supernatural agency. By the same token, there are those who believe that it is also a special reminder that the moment is of great significance and should never be forgotten. This superstitious belief has grown into a national tradition among all classes of society.

Chapter Eight:
BIZARRE
AND OTHER
EERIE SUPERSTITIONS

OMENS, CURSES & SUPERSTITIONS

Lilli Lopez, historian and folklorist, remembers in the days of her youth the ingrained belief in superstitions and omens by her grandparents and others. In her recollections, which she called: *Pineylore - Memories of my Youth*, Lopez tells about the rich traditions that everyday people in rural New Jersey led their day to day lives by.

"If Grandmom's dooryard rooster, in the forenoon, stretched and crowed, she'd shade her eyes to watch for comp'ny comin' up the road. And, if by chance a frightened bird should fly into her room, it was for her a dismal forecast of impending doom.

"Grandmom had signs and omens that seemed to rule her life. Tho' they seemed ordinary, they portended good or strife. Sometimes, the things she told us kids - we'd laugh and say, "that's funny." Like itchin' nose meant 'kiss a fool,' but itchin' hand meant 'money.'

"But we believed our brains would be improved by eating fish, and wishbones or a falling star would help us get our wish. Tho' sometimes she gave warnings foreboding to the young, one was if you lied, you'd get a blister on your tongue.

"I wondered if my friends had grannies who read signs like mine, and did she make some warnings up, to keep us kids in line. Bad luck was shoes on tables, or umbrellas raised inside. Crossed fingers stood for 'time out,' good luck, or when one lied.

"She'd say, 'It's bad luck after dark to sweep the kitchen floor, and you're sweeping out good luck if you sweep dirt out the door.' Laughter in the morning meant before dark you would cry. Your nose must pick out stitches sewn on Sunday, when you die. A sudden shiver meant someone 'walks on your grave,' she said, and when the rain is falling, then resting is the dead. A little teething babe would suffer more, alas, if somebody showed him his image in a lookin' glass.

"A knife beneath a mattress would help to 'cut' a pain. A magnet, tho, is what it took to draw out stress and strain. The breaking of a lookin' glass was good cause for alarm, tho' horseshoes hanging upside down protected homes from harm.

"An accidentally dropped fork meant a man would visit soon, but a lady was expected if, by chance, you dropped a spoon. Someone is talking 'bout you - left for love and right for spite if your ear rings in the morning; it's the opposite at night.

"Look over your left shoulder when the moon is new, and hold your open purse up prosperity will come to you. Bubbles stood for money when brimming in your cup, and it was very lucky to find a coin, heads up. To find a four leaf clover was a lucky sign, but then, fate was always lurking to rear its head again.

"It was bad luck to spill salt, but by the same accord, if you tossed some o'er your shoulder, good luck would be restored. Grandmom's signs and omens aren't repeated much these days, and tho' I don't have faith in them, I miss her mystic ways."

Follow the Signs

"Our Grandpop lived with us when I was a kid. After supper we'd take walks together to search nature's treasure. I learned many things, including the signs of the weather. In the fall he would point out the woolly worm's coats. 'There's a hard Winter time on the way jes' lookit them squirrels scurry, gatherin' nuts. They're tellin' us too,' he would say.

OMENS, CURSES & SUPERSTITIONS

"'Cornhusks are heavy; holly berries hang thick. The birds' buildin' their nests higher, too. Yes, I see Ol' Man Winters' a clinchin' his fist. Mark my words - all these signs will come true.' Sometimes he'd say, 'Mebbe we should git back. The bats and swallers fly low; they're lookin' for places to roost for a storm. It's a wonderful thing, how they know. Jes' hark at the croakin' of them ol' bullfrogs, and look at the ring around the moon. My ol' bones is achin' and that's a sure sign; yes, I 'spect we'll be gettin' rain soon.'

"In the summer he'd listen to crickets that chirped; he'd count chirps for a temperature rise. He could tell if next day would be muggy or hot by the lights and the clouds in the skies. But, late March, I believe, was our favorite time, after we'd have our share of cold spells, when the little tree frogs we called 'peepers' woke up, and we'd hark for a sound like sleigh bells.

"Down by the millpond, when leafbuds appeared, they announced the arrival of Spring, and sometimes he would show me these tiny tree frogs that swell twice the size when they sing. 'Grandpop,' I once asked, 'how did you get so wise? How do you remember so well?' "My child, everything in this world's for a cause - I jest follow the signs that they tell.'"

Lore of the South and Midwest

Mrs. Lena Bell Tyler who grew up in Tennessee, remembers that people use to tell her that it was unlucky to cut the hair of a baby until it was one year old.

Mr. and Mrs. John and Rosalie Swartz of Elwood, Indiana, say that a cat washing her face, sparks from a wood stove flying to the floor, a knife or fork falling - indicate a visit by a stranger. The first member of the assembled company at which the cat glared would be the first to die. Ringing in the ears means news. Right ear - good news, left ear - bad news. A bird trying to get into the house means that someone will soon die.

Sarah Lingwall, who was born in Alabama and lived in Tennessee, relates that in order to avoid bad luck you must exit a house from the same door you entered.

"If cows are seen lying down in the field it means that it will soon be raining," from Lee Hefley of St. Louis, Missouri.

David Jacob's paternal grandmother spent her days along the Mississippi river. She would often tell David about the old timey beliefs concerning evil spirits. The spirit could be seen as an old hag but could change form, becoming any living creature, a frog, an insect, or a black cat. Its purpose was torment; it brought about poor health, misfortune, and mischief.

One way an evil spirit could torment someone was through riding. When it wished to ride someone, a spirit entered the house of its sleeping victim, slipped a bit into their mouth and the nightmare began. You know you've been ridden when you wake up fatigued and depressed, often with bit marks at the corner of the mouth and lashes on the back from its whip.

Because the spirit plaits the victim's hair into stirrups, one way to prevent a riding is to tie your hair with thread before bed. As it must shed its skin before riding, sharp objects left in its path will thwart it by catching on its empty skin, preventing it from re-entering it.

OMENS, CURSES & SUPERSTITIONS

There is a close connection between demons and horses; therefore hanging horseshoes over windows and doors and throughout the house keeps away the unwelcome visitor. Some believe that the demon is forced to travel all the roads that the horseshoe had traveled before it could enter the house. Daylight and safety will arrive before it finished the route.

Evil spirits and demons also had a counting instinct which forced them to count all that they see. So a spirit - riding could be avoided by leaving items in its path - a sieve, it will be forced to count all the holes; a broom, it will count all the straws. Some people scattered mustard seeds or sand throughout the house. The spirit could be caught before it had time to count each grain.

Charles W. Chesnutt in a series of letters written in 1870, told how during a visit to North Carolina, he took occasion to inquire into the latter-day prevalence of the old-time belief in what was known as "conjuration" or "goopher." The name "goopher" has been lost over the years. However, the origin of this curious superstition itself is perhaps more easily traceable. It probably grew, in the first place, out of African fetishism, which was brought over from Africa.

Certain features, too, suggest a distant affinity with Voodooism, or snake worship, a cult which seems to have been indigenous to tropical America. These beliefs were mingled and confused with the witchcraft and ghost lore of the Europeans. In the old plantation days they flourished vigorously, though discouraged by the "great house," and their potency was well established among the Africans and the poorer whites.

The means of conjuration are as simple as the indications. It is a condition of all conjuring stories that there must in some way be contact, either with the person, or with some object or image intended to represent the person to be affected; or, if not actual contact, at least close proximity. The charm is placed under the door-sill, or buried under the hearth, or hidden in the mattress of the person to be conjured.

OMENS, CURSES & SUPERSTITIONS

It may be a crude attempt to imitate the body of the victim, or it may consist merely of a bottle, or a gourd, or a little bag, containing a few rusty nails, crooked pins, or horse-hairs. It may be a mysterious mixture thrown surreptitiously upon the person to be injured, or merely a line drawn across a road or path, which line it is fatal for a certain man or woman to cross. Chesnutt told of a laboring man who went two miles out of his way, every morning and evening, while going to and from his work, to avoid such a line drawn for him by a certain powerful enemy.

Some of the more gruesome phases of the belief in conjuration suggest possible poisoning. The blood or venom of snakes, spiders, and lizards is supposed to be employed for this purpose. The results of its administration are so peculiar, however, and so entirely improbable, that one is supposed to doubt even the initial use of poison, and figure it in as part of the same general delusion. For instance, a certain man "swelled up all over" and became "pieced," that is, pied or spotted.

A white physician who was summoned thought that the man thus singularly afflicted was poisoned, but did not recognize the poison nor know the antidote. A conjure doctor, was subsequently called in and more prompt in his diagnosis. The man, he said, was poisoned with a lizard, which at that very moment was lodged somewhere in the, patient's anatomy.

This lizard, according to the conjure doctor, would start from the man's shoulder, descend to his hand, return to the shoulder, and pass down the side of the body to the leg. When it reached the calf of the leg the lizard's head would appear right under the skin. After it had been perceptible for three days the lizard was to be cut out with a razor, or the man would die. Sure enough, the lizard manifested its presence in the appointed place at the appointed time; but the patient would not permit the surgery, and at the end of three days passed away.

OMENS, CURSES & SUPERSTITIONS

Comets, Superstitions, and Mark Twain

In *"The Return of Halley's Comet,"* published in the ***American Monthly Review of Reviews*** in April of 1910, S. A. Mitchell noted some of the widely-held superstitions about comets: Those who remember the great comet of 1882 will recall that many said that it was the cause of the war that England was then carrying on in Egypt; and our own great Civil War was ushered in by Donati's splendid comet of 1858, and by the comets of 1860 and 1861. Such coincidences can be counted over and over; and it is natural that there should have grown up in the popular mind down through the centuries the conviction that a comet brought in its train disasters of all kinds. Including, war, murder, and sudden death.

In Inventing Mark Twain: ***The Lives of Samuel Langhorne Clemens***, Andrew Hoffman interprets the arrival of Halley's Comet in 1835 as a sign of good luck, "the most auspicious element in the child's birth." However, people seem to have more frequently viewed comets as a sign of impending danger. It is more likely that the comet was blamed for Twain's premature birth, he arrived two months early and, weighing only five pounds, had little chance for survival. As the months passed, though, the comet may well have been remembered more favorably, providing an explanation for his improving health.

The next comet in Twain's life coincided with a similarly mixed event. Twain saw Donati's Comet in June of 1858, the month his brother Henry died from injuries suffered in the explosion of the **Pennsylvania** on the Mississippi River below Memphis. Twain was working on that boat with his brother and might also have died in the explosion if he had not left the ship in New Orleans just eight days before after fighting with its pilot.

Twain's experiences with comets can certainly be interpreted with the superstitions about their effects that were widely held while he was alive, but not without a little

93

fudging. He survived a premature birth and was away from danger when the **Pennsylvania** exploded. Failing health in 1909 must have contributed to the accuracy of his prediction that he would die the following year when Halley's Comet returned, but before that Mark Twain managed to live through the disasters that accompanied the comets in his life.

Chapter Nine:
CALLING UPON
THE FOUR CORNERS
OF THE WORLD

OMENS, CURSES & SUPERSTITIONS

One of the things that hold us as human beings together, is the universal belief of omens, curses, and superstitions. No matter where you travel, you are sure to find some belief that would be considered superstition. Superstitions seem to strike a familiar cord in our unconscious minds, and that is why we find their continued existance.

Russian Superstitions

The Russian culture is very interesting and very complex. To foreigners it may seem even more confusing as to why Russians do certain things. While an American will walk around a ladder without even thinking about it, to some it may seem a bit odd even humorous to see a Russian priest rolling around in a field of sprouting crops. There are many other occurrences which may seem strange if you are not Russian but keep in mind many of the things we do today would seem strange to foreigners.

The reason that the priests roll around in the fields is because this is supposed to bring fertility to the land. In the Ukraine on St. George's Day (April 23) married couples do the rolling in the fields and the priest only blesses the crops.

In Southern Russia the children there, when they lose a tooth, throw it on the roof and ask a mouse to give them an iron tooth in exchange for their bone tooth. This may seem funny but Americans ask for money from a fairy when they lose teeth.

If you are a foreigner traveling through Southern Russia, you'd best hope they're not going through a drought. In Kursk, a province in Southern Russia, the women in the village seize a stranger and proceed to throw him in the river. This helps to bring rain.

OMENS, CURSES & SUPERSTITIONS

Russians also will not have their silhouettes cut because they will surely die before the year is out. It is a good idea to go to church on Palm Sunday. If you don't you could get an "Easter Smack." The Russians beat their children and servants with palm sticks believing that it will make them healthy and put "health into their bones."

On September first, Russian girls make coffins for flies and other insects. Included in the coffins are turnips and other vegetables. They then bury the coffin and mourn it as if it were their mother. This is supposed to get rid of the insects so that the harvest will be good.

The reason that Russian brides wear a fishing net over them is because the knots on the net will keep them from any harm they might be faced with. Knots were a defense against sorcerers. The Russian wood spirits were called Ljeschie, from the word ljes meaning wood. These are spirits of wood and corn and are similar to humans but have horns, legs and ears of a goat. This may seem scary but keep in mind that they can change form whenever they please.

On New Year's Day, in Eastern Russia, in order to get rid of the demons Russians beat every inch of their homes and yard with sticks. Each stick is split in nine different places. While they beat the house and yard they say, "We are driving Satan out of the village." The sticks are then thrown into the river and float downstream to the next village where they must repeat the procedure.

In the United States we smoke cigars at the birth of a child. In Russia they plant a tree. This tree grows with the child and if it flourishes so will the child. Likewise if it dwindles so will the child. Therefore, these trees are taken very good care of. This belief that the tree and the child are connected is believed not only in Russia but also in Germany, England, France and Italy.

OMENS, CURSES & SUPERSTITIONS

Thieves in Russia will murder a girl and then use her for making candles of human tallow. They hope that this will allow them to pursue their victims without being seen.

On the Eve of St. John, Russian men and young women jump over the bonfire in couples. Sometimes they even drive their cattle through the fire because this will protect them from wizards and witches who are hungry for their milk.

The villagers in Russia in order to protect themselves against epidemics would draw a furrow around the village. This was believed to prevent any unclean spirits from passing through.

Although many of the Russian superstitions seem strange they do have their reasons. Whether based in ancient myth or the Christian church, there is a belief behind every action. In order to better understand the Russian culture we must first understand the reasons behind the actions.

Chinese New Year Superstitions

Most Chinese superstitions surround the celebration of Chinese New Year, even though some of these superstitions concern everyday life. Here are just some of these superstitions.

Long ago, there was a monster called Nian. It ate many humans from a little village. Nian came once a year and would always wreak havoc to all the villagers. One day, the villagers found out that the monster was actually afraid of the color red and noise. Thus, to many Chinese, the color red signifies joy and luck and that it is an auspicious color for all festive occasions whereas the black color is an unlucky color.

OMENS, CURSES & SUPERSTITIONS

Spring cleaning before the Chinese New Year is also very important as it is believed that good fortune favors a clean house and fortune would smile on a family which is clean. Sweeping during Chinese New Year is counted unlucky as you would be sweeping the luck out of your house.

The Kitchen God is the most important of the domestic deities. Before Chinese New Year, he receives offerings from people, then he would present his annual report about the behavior of the household to the Jade Emperor. Sweet stuffs are often offered so that the Kitchen God's words would be sweet and flattering.

During visiting, mandarin oranges are exchanged because in Cantonese, both the word orange and gold have the same pronunciation which is also synonymous to "sweetness." Thus, oranges are thought to bring sweetness and wealth when offered in pairs.

New year goodies also have significant meanings. Nian Gao is a circular brown cake made of flour and sugar. The word Gao has the same pronunciation as the word "high" in mandarin, so whoever eats the `nian gao` will attain a higher status or ascend to a better life in the new year.

Tobago Folklore: Superstitions in Agriculture and Fishing

When there is a funeral in the village you must not go into your garden to plant. Yams, especially Ibo yams, are very sensitive plants and correspondingly require special treatment: Both men and women must bathe well before entering a yam plot. Women who are flowering (having their monthly periods) must never enter a yam plot while that condition exists. When attending to all yam plots it is advisable to abstain from sexual intercourse as long as that exercise is in progress.

OMENS, CURSES & SUPERSTITIONS

Never sell or give away your planting material before you have completed your own planting. Sweet potatoes should not be planted during the month of August because the tubers produce close to the surface regardless of soil conditions and depth of planting. Many tubers will emerge from the soil, dry-up and spoil before maturity. If two coconut seedlings are planted the final height can be determined at planting. A seedling that is planted while the planter is seated and during the full and last quarter moon phases will be considerably shorter at fruiting than another plant which was planted with the planter standing and during the new moon and first quarter moon phases.

Over the years, there has evolved among the fisherfolk of Tobago, numerous superstitions. These vary in some respects from beach to beach. Many of these superstitions are based on things which may bring either good or bad luck to the fishermen's fishing activities.

A fisherman should not wash his hands with soap before going to sea. It is thought that by washing his hands his luck would be washed away. A fisherman should not play with animals such as goats, sheep, pigs, dogs, donkeys, or cows before going to sea. Doing this is supposed to cause the fisherman ill luck during his fishing trip.

Sexual intercourse before going to sea is supposed to bring bad luck. Touching chive before going to sea is held to bring bad luck. Some fishermen believe that spraying their boats with oils and ointments will bring them good luck when they go to sea. Other fishermen believe in using bushes and lime to 'bathe' their boats and their bodies. This is supposed to remove any bad luck attached to their boats or their persons.

OMENS, CURSES & SUPERSTITION

Japanese Superstitions

An American would probably laugh at the thought of a snake bringing a fortune of unexpected money. An American wouldn't worry about being in the middle of a photograph with two other people in it. An American would probably call anyone who believed in such things superstitious. But then, is that the type of person who would avoid opening an umbrella in the house? Does that person worry when he sees a black cat coming his way? These are things that a Japanese person would laugh at, just as you may have laughed at their superstitions.

The Japanese believe in many creatures relating to myths. One of the most famous is "oni", or devil. They occasionally have three eyes and are almost always giant sized. Their colors are red, blue, grey or pink. They have horns. Three toes and three fingers are unusual features that Oni's have. They have the ability to fly, but hardly ever do. They are dumb, cruel, and malicious. Most myths relate to a religion, whether it is Buddhism, Shinto, or a different religion.

The Japanese have their own ghosts. Their ghosts are different from ours because all that we really think of as ghosts are clear little white things. Their ghosts each have their own personality and ways to terrorize people. Some general terms for ghosts are "obake" or "bakemono." That literally means transforming thing. "youkai" means bewitching apparition, which includes monsters, goblins, and ghouls.

"Yuurei" is a dim, hazy, or faint spirit. These are probably the closest types of ghosts to America's vision of them that you will get. They are supposedly dead spirits living on earth for a reason. An example of youkai is "Rokurokubi," a female monster with a long, flexible neck. She looks like a regular woman during the day, but at night, she takes all of their energy away from them, and they die. Women ghosts come back in taxi cabs, and other ghosts come back as cats.

OMENS, CURSES & SUPERSTITIONS

Long ago, there were many superstitions, but, as in all cultures, they have began to die out. Japan has very interesting superstitions, possibly because they are so different from the familiar western superstitions. The Japanese have charms, days, numbers, directions and death all incorporated into superstitions.

The fourth and fourteenth days of a month are considered unlucky, while the fifteenth and 28th days are thought of as lucky days. Lucky days are good for starting projects and trips. The numbers four, nine, and thirteen are considered unlucky. Four means death, nine means pain, and thirteen is basically just the result of American superstitions. In a hospital, it is very uncommon to see rooms numbered four, nine, fourteen, or 42 because they are all somehow associated with death or pain. In the maternity section of hospital, the room numbered 43 is avoided because it literally means still birth.

Many Japanese superstitions are associated with death. For example, you should never stick your chopsticks straight up and down in your rice bowl because that is how it is done at a death. You should always lay out your futon so it is pointed south. Your pillow should never point north. This is the position of a body of a dead person at a Buddhist funeral. Some superstitions are considered foolish and funny, but those concerning death are taken very seriously.

Whether we believe ourselves to be superstitious or not, in truth, we are bound up within a profound web of ancient lore that operates within our subconscious minds. These memories are the memories of our most distant ancestors and the world which they inhabited. Belief in omens and superstitions remain as outward expressions of the tensions and anxieties that hold sway over mankind as it struggles down the corridor of life from birth to death, buffeted by change and uncertainty.

Chapter Ten:
LADY SUZANNE'S FAVORITE SPELLS AND RITUALS -- LEARN TO GET WHAT YOU WANT AND PROTECT YOURSELF

OMENS, CURSES & SUPERSTITIONS

Now that you've read about the possible jinxes, curses, omens and negative superstitions that can possibly be thrown at you, or cross your path, you'll be more anxious than ever to manifest some good luck.

Obviously, we're all looking for luck in our personal life, be it material, spiritual or love related. We're also looking for protection against that which can do us, our family and closest friends the most harm. Many are searching - - some more desperately than others - - for a "way out" of their current bind.

I am pleased to be able to offer what may seem like a rare glimmer of hope many of you reading this book so rightfully deserve. The next few pages should be more than helpful in offering what we seek the most toward creating good luck in a protected environment.

Make Your Own Luck

In the end, we all make our own luck. Sure we can go to others and get their advice and pay them to bless us or to do a spell. Sometimes this works, but the very best spells are the ones you put your own intent and energy into.

In my own work, I take a slightly different slant on luck than a lot of other practicing occultists do, as well as on the manifestation of good luck when working with others to accomplish their desired goals. If you are experiencing what you perceive as bad luck, what you need to do is to shake up your surroundings and the energy that surrounds your physical, astral, and emotional bodies.

The best time to do a spell for purposes of good luck would be when the planet Mars rules the heavens - - which would be on Tuesday. In calculating the best times, the first, eighth, thirteenth and twenty second hour after midnight are the hours governed by Mars. This translates into midnight, 7AM, 2PM, and 10PM. For the very best results you will want to work when the Moon is between new and full. (Known as the waxing Moon).

The first thing you will need to do is to set up an altar or ritual table facing east. Clean the table or altar using salt and collect as many items that you can find that represent in your mind good luck. Feel free to include any items you may already have in your possession. Look around you and gather all that you consider lucky. If you don't immediately see anything then it should be fairly easy to comprehend how you can change your environmental influences by changing the things with which you surround yourself.

Fast Luck Ritual

For this ritual I suggest you assemble the following ingredients in the fast luck ritual:

- One orange candle.

- One "seven knobbed" green candle.

- Two white "seven day" candles.

- One astral candle corresponding to your astrological sign.

- Fast luck incense.

- Charcoal.

- Salt.

- Buckeye.

- Hi John Root.

- Lo John Root.

- Lodestone.

- Tonka or African Mojo Beans.

- Lucky Hand Root.

- Dragons Blood Powder.

- Devil's Shoe String.

- One piece of Jade.

- An Amazonite stone.

- Glass of water

- Green colored Mojo bag.

105

Set up your alter as shown
in the illustration below.

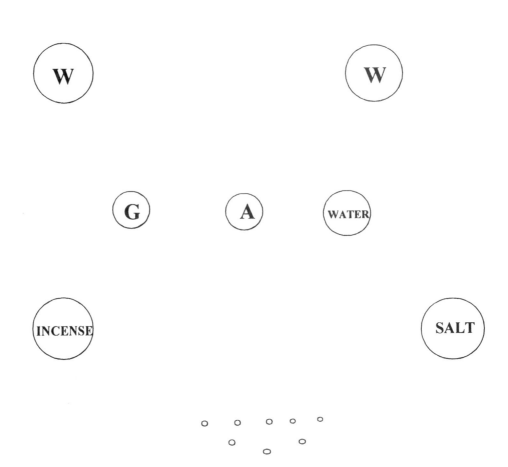

Ingredients

OMENS, CURSES & SUPERSTITIONS

Before starting the ritual take a bath in salt water. Let yourself dry in the air while visualizing the water and your impurities going down the drain. Make a circle of salt starting in the east, going clockwise around the room. Light your white candles and your incense. Then light your astral candle (see chart); the orange candle and the green candle - - in that order. While the first knob of the green candle burns take each candle and pass them through the incense smoke while repeating the following invocation:

As these things pass through the smoke all the powers I invoke.
Powers that change my fate. Come to me and congregate.
Don't hesitate to do my will . . . Change my luck with perfect skill.
Protect me from my enemy for as my will so it must be!

Place the assembled items in the green Mojo bag, breathe into the bag three times and say:

With my breath this change I lay.
My luck will change in every way.
This lucky bag alive for me.
And as my will so it be.

Close the bag, tie three knots in the string and carry it with you. Hold it in your left hand to receive luck. Hold it in your right hand to send it to others. Burn one knob of the green candle every night at 10 PM for a week. Let the other candles burn down.

Say out loud in a commanding voice :

IT IS DONE ! IT MUST BE !

OMENS, CURSES & SUPERSTITIONS

ASTRAL CANDLE COLORS

SIGN	DATES	1st COLOR	2nd COLOR
Aquarius	Jan. 20 - Feb 18	Blue	Green
Pisces	Feb 19 - Mar 20	White	Green
Aries	Mar 21 - April 19	White	Pink
Taurus	April 20 - May 20	Red	Yellow
Gemini	May 21- June 21	Red	Blue
Cancer	June 22 - July 22	Green	Brown
Leo	July 23 - Aug 22	Red	Green
Virgo	Aug 23 - Sept 22	Gold	Black
Libra	Sept 23 - Oct 22	Black	Blue
Scorpio	Oct 23 - Nov 21	Brown	Black
Sagittarius	Nov 22 - Dec 21	Gold	Red
Capricorn	Dec 22 - Jan 19	Red	Brown

If you cannot find the first astral color for yourself or others involved in the spell, feel free to use the second candle that is given in the above list. Dress your alter candles with candle dressing oil or sandalwood oil if you can't find altar oil locally.

OMENS, CURSES & SUPERSTITIONS

Here is a wonderful ritual to change your luck. Find a small chamois bag, preferably one with a cord long enough so that you can wear the bag around your neck. Inside this bag place - - in order to attract what you wish to attract - - lodestone; a piece of High John root; one buckeye; a piece of Devil's Shoe String and some five finger grass or a Lucky Hand root. Assemble all these items on a Thursday during the waxing moon in the 1st, 8th, 15th or 22nd hour after midnight. Light a candle anointed with Fast Luck Oil and allow it to burn down during this hour while burning Good Luck Drawing or Fast Luck Incense.

Next you must pass the bag through the smoke and then pass each of the assembled items through the incense smoke while reciting the following invocation:

Bag and herbs this charge I lay...
That there remain within your frame.
No adverse through,
no enmity,
and as my will so it will be!

Let seven drops of the candle wax fall into the open bag and insert each root of herb while visualizing your luck changing. When you come to the Devil's Shoe String, concentrate on anything that would be an obstacle to your good luck, then break the Devil's Shoe String in half and know the snapping of the root is also breaking up those obstacles. Place the pieces in the bag. Hold the bag in your left hand to receive luck. Or hold the bag in your right hand to send it to someone you love. Wear the bag around your neck to insure good luck comes your way.

Lady Suzanne's Spell for Personal Protection

How do you know when you are under psychic attack? And what do you do when you feel this situation occurring? Believe me, you'll find yourself challenged and attacked by forces that are not even visible. The attacks are, in a sense, as obstacles that you must overcome.

OMENS, CURSES & SUPERSTITIONS

You can choose to be blocked until you evolve to a level high enough to navigate around the situation. You can blast through it with sheer force of will, or you can seek to understand it. In order to block these situations, you will need to master the art of protection. Some of your best friends, or "allies," in this fight are YOUR OWN WILL, STRENGTH and SPIRIT.

ITEMS REQUIRED: Salt - Black rocks - Your own breath - Bells, chimes, drums and mirrors - Fringe - An appropriate protection amulet or talisman - Tassels Protection incense - Sage.

To start the ritual, face east and sprinkle salt in a circle around your premises. Bathe in it. Swim in it. The circles of salt around your premises or room can get smaller as you feel the need. Mix salt and water and sprinkle it around each room and it can be done anytime. It is a ritual all by itself and can help with protection from negative forces or astral attack.

Mix it in your chalice. In a crystal glass or in a container of any kind, but keep in mind that the more salt you use the more pleasing the results will be to yourself. Here is the essential part of this ritual: Breathe over the container and visualize your own breath as being electric blue light. Make little ripples in the water as you feel the heat of your breath empowering the liquid. See the liquid glowing. Empower it to form a protective barrier on everything it touches. When you feel you are protected, big things will come into your life, and you will suddenly feel good about others who surround you as well as your personal surroundings.

I've created these rituals especially for this book. If you follow them with inner strength, energy and enthusiasm, they will lead to a safer, luckier life. Blessed Be.